WORDLE LIMERICKS

FLAMERICKS

Volume 1

By Marshall S Flam, MD

Copyright © 2025 Marshall S Flam

All rights reserved. No part of this book may be reproduced, stored, or transmitted by any means—whether auditory, graphic, mechanical, or electronic—without written permission of both publisher and author, except in the case of brief excerpts used in critical articles and reviews. Unauthorized reproduction of any part of this work is illegal and is punishable by law.

ISBN: 979-8-89419-385-4 (sc)
ISBN: 979-8-89419-386-1 (hc)
ISBN: 979-8-89419-387-8 (e)

Because of the dynamic nature of the Internet, any web addresses or links contained in this book may have changed since publication and may no longer be valid. The views expressed in this work are solely those of the author and do not necessarily reflect the views of the publisher, and the publisher hereby disclaims any responsibility for them.

For more information, visit:
www.wordlelimericks.net
www.wordlelimericks.com

One Galleria Blvd., Suite 1900, Metairie, LA 70001
(504) 702-6708

I hope this book you'll not spurn

And your full attention I will earn

My Limericks won't make you cry

So go ahead give them a try

And join with me to LAUGH & LEARN

ENJOY!

INTRODUCTION

WORDLE LIMERICKS
"FLAMERICKS"

It was during my early teenage years that I discovered the limerick. Of course, the majority of those that I encountered over the next 60 years were obscene, which made them more titillating for a young man to enjoy. It was extremely rare to encounter a limerick that was not obscene or at least bawdry although, admittedly, I doubt that I ever searched for any. I clearly recall standing at a neighborhood street corner in the Bronx with friends, creating limericks off the tops of our heads, laughing and then rapidly forgetting them.

With my later discovery of *The Limerick 1700 Examples with Notes Variants and Index*, edited by G. Legman and published in 1964, I was able to enjoy many more vulgar, bawdy, obscene, lewd, filthy, and profane five-line wonders than I ever considered possible.

In the introduction to Legman's compilation of limericks, La Cle des Champs opines that "the clean limerick has never been of the slightest interest to anyone since the end of its brief fad in the 1860s"[1]. Until recently, I would have also subscribed to this narrow viewpoint. The new online game, Wordle, changed that opinion for me, and I hope after reading my Wordle-associated limericks (Wordle Limericks or Flamericks), you will come to agree.

The limerick as a poem form originated in England in the early years of the 18th century. Although the specific origins remain unknown, it has been suggested that the name derives from the chorus of an 18th-century Irish soldier's song: "Will You Come Up to Limerick". The earliest forms of the limerick were short rhyming poems used by the working class and drunkards. Although many limericks innocently began as children's nursery rhymes, once they were adopted by those under the influence of alcohol, the connotation was forever changed. The British working class, although illiterate, could easily remember five lines of a catchy limerick during a period of relaxation (often in a pub) through laughter after a hard day's work.

Historically, Saint Thomas Aquinas (1225-1274) wrote the first limerick in the 13th century. His five-line rhyming verse penned in medieval Latin appears to be the oldest surviving example of this poetic form. In 1845, Edward Lear published *The Book of Nonsense*, which featured 72 limericks. This was the first collection of limericks ever published. This book also included illuminating

---

[1] Legman, G. (1964). The Limerick. Bell Publishing Company.

illustrations associated with the limericks. Lear updated this work in 1872. In total, he wrote and published 212 nonsense limericks.

The limerick form consists of 5 lines in the rhyming pattern of AABBA. The first, second-, and fifth lines end in words that rhyme with each other, while the third and fourth lines end in words that rhyme with each other but not (necessarily) with lines 1, 2, and 5. Lines 1, 2, and 5 are longer than lines 3 and 4 and have roughly the same number of syllables (usually 8 to 10). Lines 3 and 4 are shorter, each with the same number of syllables but with fewer syllables (usually 5 to 6) than lines 1, 2, and 5. Another way to express this is lines 1,2, and 5 are trimeter lines (da da da/ da da da/da da da), while lines 3 and 4 are shorter dimeter lines (da da da/ da da da).

These short poems create humorous and vivid imagery. They are usually outrageous, connecting thoughts and phrases that are unusual and often unexpected which, when juxtaposed, prove to be marginally to outrageously funny. The fifth and final line is the punchline, which arrives after an evolving set up. Thus, the limerick is, in essence, a short 5-line poem with just one stanza.

In creating these limericks, I have done my utmost to adhere to this classical structure. Where my Wordle Limericks (Flamericks) might occasionally differ is in the addition of a sixth line which will rhyme with lines 1, 2, and 5. These additional lines will be embraced by parenthesis. This 6th line might emphasize the ending, provide an alternative or contradictory meaning, or serve as the punchline.

Many of my limericks are intended to be educational and/or informational. Therefore, many are accompanied by explanatory footnotes in a dedicated portion following the limerick(s) section. Footnotes are indicated by an asterisk (*) which represents an invitation to the reader to turn to the corresponding footnote number to enhance their understanding of the limerick and perhaps learn something they did not know or might have forgotten. As my intention with many limericks is to educate, when there are occasions where the 3rd and/or 4th lines are of greater length than the classical dimeter, I will let this stand, as I would rather make the educational point than sacrifice it to strict adherence to conventional rules.

In summary, Wordle Limericks differ from conventional limericks as follows:

1. The subject is triggered by the daily word of the internet game Wordle.
2. They do not have to be bawdry, but they may be so.
3. A sixth line (or more) can be added in trimeter fashion that rhymes with lines 1, 2, and 5.
4. Perfect adherence to the conventional length is not strictly enforced if it sacrifices an opportunity to educate, enlighten, or amuse.
5. Any subject matter is allowable.
6. Explanatory footnotes are used when needed.

Where I have written more than one limerick for a Wordle word, they are frequently unrelated. On occasion, they are connected as a continuation of a story initiated in the first limerick or as an elaboration of a concept. Unrelated limericks of the same Wordle word will be separated by numbers in a bracket such as (1), (2), (3), and so on. No separation symbol will be employed between connected sequential limericks.

Wordle is a web-based game created and developed by Josh Wardle, a software engineer. A player has six opportunities to guess the correct five-letter word on each calendar day. It was developed because he and his partner loved word games. The first Wordle word "CIGAR" (#0) was released on June 21, 2021. After the couple played for a few months, it rapidly became an obsession in their small WhatsApp social network. It was released to the public in October of 2021, after Wardle added the ability for players to copy their daily results as emoji squares, which were widely shared on Twitter. He sold the game to the New York Times on January 31, 2022, for a "price in the low seven figures" (^{2}).

The game was launched online for the public in October 2021 with fewer than 100 players in its early weeks. Currently, between 2 and 3 million people worldwide play it. There are 12,986 recognized five letter words in the English language. The Wordle game allows a total of 2,309 five-letter words as solution words. (These do not include plurals, names, or words in the past tense, though they are allowed as guesses, just not as solutions.) Consequently, the last Wordle word will be offered on October 14, 2027. This will allow me to potentially publish an estimated total of 8 to 10 volumes of limericks.

By the time I discovered Wordle, there had been 312 words played. I started playing Wordle on April 28, 2022, with the word ZESTY. I quickly became addicted and shared my results with a small number of friends and family. Five months later, on October 2, 2022, I began writing limericks each day that incorporated the daily Wordle word and based the subject of the limerick upon that specific word. My first Wordle Limerick was #470 (TWINE). I soon discovered that this was an extremely enjoyable pastime, and the few individuals with whom I shared the Wordle Limericks found them quite entertaining and looked forward to reading them. After a while, the creation of the daily limericks became of greater importance to me than the number of guesses it took for me to discover the word of the day. Over time, the nature of the limericks became wide-ranging. While some were traditionally obscene, the bulk were not. I began to see these small gems in a novel light, with their envisioned purpose being not only to amuse but also to educate, encourage contemplation, rekindle memories and feelings, and perhaps raise enough interest in a particular limerick to stimulate further research.

As I started composing Wordle Limericks on #470, I was forced to go back and write at least one limerick for the preceding 469 Wordle words, retroactively. I managed to close the gap and now write an average of 5 limericks for each word, daily. This first edition employs Wordle words #0-400 for which I have composed 607 limericks. The second volume will employ #s 401-800, for a grand total of 998 limericks representing the first 801 Wordle words to be represented in Volumes 1 and 2.

---

[2] Cunnigham, A. (2022, January 31). "New York Times spends "low seven figures' ' to buy Wordle". arsTECHNICA. https://arstechnica.com/gaming/2022/01/whats-a-five-letter-word-for-acquire-nyt-buys-wordle-for-low-7-figures/

This Volume is a republication of the limericks representing the first 401 Wordle words that was originally self-published on December 15, 2023. Many of the original limericks have been modified and refined, while many have had additional sixth lines added thanks to my granddaughter's particular skill in this arena.

I hope you will enjoy reading my limericks as much as I have enjoyed creating them. I hope that this unusual format will broaden your horizons despite the infrequence of its conventional bawdry humour. Try reading them out loud with family and friends to enhance your appreciation of them. As I plan to continue to write these little poems until October of 2027, it is apparent that all of them will not fit into a single volume. I have chosen to place 607 limericks based on the first 401 Wordle words in this first re-edition. Words beyond this group will be explored in upcoming volumes of this series, so stay tuned.

I hope you enjoy laughing while learning.

Marshall S Flam, MD

FOREWORD

Hi there! I'm Ralph, a gal with a goofy name. My grandfather (the infamous Marshall) and I talk on the phone about every two weeks. After finding out we both enjoy the daily Wordle, a phenomenon that hit the World(le) in full force in 2022, we started sharing our results with each other, along with a little pun about the word. Don't worry, you weren't pun-ished if you didn't get it. ☺ Groan all you want, because that's where the fun starts! (When you're all groan up.)

On Sunday, October 2, 2022, I shared "There was an Old Man of Thermopylae" by Edward Lear with my grandfather (thank goodness for text history, am I right?). I'm subscribed to The Poetry Foundation's daily poem and, knowing his enjoyment of the lime-rich (say it out loud) culture, I shared it with him. (To which he responded "Unfortunately, it is not filthy".) See how far he's come!

And so it began. *Triumphant music.* With the next Wordle (#470 TWINE, which he got in an impressive (or lucky) two guesses), he created his first Wordle Limerick:

> "There once was a man from Lyme
> With a woman became entwined
> When she sat on his face[1]
> It was quite a disgrace
> Some consider it a sexual crime"
> (Others are more than willing to pass the time)

Okay, I might have added that last line.

I think this limerick is neat because it shows his starting point, before he transitioned from bawdry preferences to a desire to educate and exercise the mind.

It isn't really known when the first limerick originated. My grandfather elaborates more fully in his introduction, but I'm hoping someone named Rick was involved, just to satiate my punny preferences. Funnily enough, Edward Lear, the writer of the limerick I shared with my grandfather, was the man who truly popularized the phenomenon in the mid to late 19th century. As my grandfather previously mentioned, Lear published a book of limericks called "The Book of Nonsense," and I imagine Dr Suess is rather miffed he didn't come up with that himself.

My grandfather shared that limericks are meant to have a specific cadence and rhyme scheme: five lines with three-beat measures (trimeter) in the first, second, and fifth lines, and two-beat

---

[1] (Later changed to: "When her lust his outpaced").

measures (dimeter) in the third and fourth lines. As always with art, there are deviations from the norm. Limericks can be doubled to have 10 lines, be replies to other limericks, or even be extended with an extra line. You've probably got a spare napkin and a pen somewhere; give it a try!

An example, and one of my grandfather's favourites is as follows:

> "In the Garden of Eden lay Adam
> Complacently stroking his madam,
> And loud was his mirth
> For on all of the earth
> There were only two balls -- and he had 'em."

This can be found in William S. Baring-Gould's *The Lure of the Limerick*, published in 1967.

And don't worry! If you're not looking for a dirty delve into the limerick world, he provides a wide variety outside of that realm. You want historical? We've got you covered. You want it ridiculous? Here we are! You want a limerick where a fellow forgoes a steak for a cake? Have at it! (Number 22(2).) A limerick can be about anything! For example, one of my favourites from childhood went as follows:

There was an old man with a beard,
who said, "It is just as I feared!—
Two Owls and a Hen,
Four Larks and a Wren,
Have all built their nests in my beard!

This is from Edward Lear's *Book of Nonsense* (1845). In particular, I remember the illustrations. Another one from the same book that I remember fondly is:

*There was a Young lady whose chin
resembled the point of a pin;
So she had it made sharp,
And purchased a harp,
And played several tunes with her chin.*

In case you're wondering: yes, my grandfather has in fact written limericks for every single Wordle word since it was released. Each morning, I get a text that I can't read until I've solved the Wordle myself. How nice it is to have a little spark of fun to look forward to! I hope you feel the same. What you are reading here is the second publication of the first collection, based on the first 401 words. Dip your toe in (maybe not literally)! Flip to a random page! Laugh, cry, or do that little nose exhale that means you're slightly amused! If you're not sure where to start, a few of my favourites are #32 (HELIX), 93(2) (GAMMA), 115 (THUMB), 148 (PITHY), 160(2) CLOCK, 167(1) GRIME, and 231 (ALOFT).

Thank you for keeping us company as you learn about limericks and Wordle, and now the Wordle Limerick (Grandpa thought to call them Flamericks). Thank you also for surviving some fabulous puns (this is the pun-ultimate one, I promise). I hope this book brings you many laughs and much joy. Enjoy your Wordle Limericks (or Wordlimericks), and- oh my, would you look at the clock! It's time for me to book it! (And for you to book in!)

Safe reading,

Ralph 🌸

P.S. Yoo hoo! I wrote this sometime last year, for my grandfather's first publication. For his second publication, he edited his introduction a bit to describe the way that the limerick rhythm works. In it, he describes the rhythm as such: "lines 1, 2, and 5 are trimeter lines (da da da/ da da da/da da da), while lines 3 and 4 are shorter dimeter lines (da da da/ da da da)".

Now here's the important bit, peeps and squeaks. When he's doing his presentation, he actually says that whole rhythmic bit out loud! If any of you lovely folks out there ever get to hear him do a lecture on this book, please bring a top hat and cane and give it to him before the show. If you do, he will wear it while doing a tap dance routine and saying the rhythmic pattern. Can't you just see it? I made him promise! Don't fail me now, friends! Let's make Fred Astaire and Ginger Rogers turn in their tombs, or at least giggle from the grave! (Sorry, I had to do that, for alliteration purposes.)

On a very different note, I'm reminded of the fun I've had with Grandpa as we throw ideas at each other, trying to be as ridiculous as possible and make each other laugh. I'm sincerely very grateful for how goofy and fun he is, with me and in general. I feel very lucky to have such a connection with him.

Whenever we're together, we'll talk about random things and now, 93.2% of the time (don't ask about the math), he says "You know, I have a limerick for that". It's become such a joke in our family that I even made him a sticker. (I wanted to turn it into a pin, but do you have any idea how hard it is to find someone that will just make *one rectangular pin?*) Anyway, here it is, for your amusement:

Really, I'm just here to say that I love him and that I'm glad I got to do this funny little project with him. Now all that's left to say is that I hope you enjoy yourself, with this book and in life in general. I hope you have something that makes you smile today. I'll leave you with an awful(ly fantastic) dad joke, just to get things started:

Why did the pirate cut off his left hand?

Because after he cut off his right, he was *hooked*!

I'll see myself out.

CATEGORIES OF WORDLE LIMERICKS

1. ANIMALS
2. ANTHROPOLOGY/ARCHAELOGY
3. ART/ARCHITECTURE
4. CRIME/JUSRISPRUDENCE
5. DANCE
6. FAMILY/FRIENDS
7. FANTASIES/LEGENDS/TALES/MYTHS/FABLES/NURSERY RHYMES
8. FOOD/DRINK/COOKING/DIET
9. GEOGRAPHY/EXPLORATION
10. GRAMMAR/LINGUISTICS/POEMS/LIMERICKS
11. HISTORY: AMERICAN
12. HISTORY: ANCIENT
13. HISTORY: WORLD
14. HORROR/OCCULT/ETHEREAL/MAGIC
15. INSECTS/MICROBES
16. JEWELRY/FASHION
17. LITERATURE/WRITERS
18. MARRIAGE/DIVORCE/RELATIONSHIPS
19. MATHEMATICS
20. MEDICINE
21. MILITARY
22. MOVIES/THEATER/TELEVISION/RADIO
23. MUSIC
24. PERSONALITIES
25. PHILOSOPHY
26. POLITICS/ECONOMICS
27. PSYCHOLOGY/PSYCHIATRY
28. RELIGIOUS/BIBLICAL
29. ROYALTY
30. SCIENCE/TECHNOLOGY/GEOLOGY/ASTRONOMY
31. SPORTS
32. SEXUAL/OBSCENE/BAWDRY
33. UNCLASSIFIABLE

0. CIGAR - 19 JUNE 2021

Bill Clinton certainly got very far
Only few could achieve on his par
But the Lewinsky scandal*
Was more than he could handle
He had no clue what to do with a cigar
(Proved he couldn't control his cigar)

1. REBUT - 20 JUNE 2021
See 35(2) PAPER

Upon discovery of the tomb of King Tut*
His sarcophagus was found tightly shut
After letting in air
And yelling in his ear
Poor Tut was still unable to **rebut**

2. SISSY - 21 JUNE 2021

It doesn't take much to be a **sissy**
All you need is a fit that is hissy
A bit of pixie dust
A dash of ditzy fuss
And someone to call you prissy

3. HUMPH - 22 JUNE 2021
See 87 GOLEM

The Golem* moved with a galumph
Threatening all with a big harumph
When his clay fell apart
It was with gleeful heart
That I muttered a bewildered **humph**
(I'm still not certain it was a triumph)

4. AWAKE - 23 JUNE 2021

There was a young man named Jake
Who once made a terrible mistake
Proposing to his gal
Was completely irrational
For at that moment she wasn't **awake**
(All it gave him was a bellyache)

5. BLUSH - 24 JUNE 2021

Cindy was a strange kind of lush
Who when sober would always **blush**
She was so absent minded
She had to be reminded
Not to fix her hair with a toothbrush

Her accommodations were very plush
But that never made her **blush**
Despite her high bound airs
She drove her maid to tears
By forgetting her toilet to flush

6. FOCAL - 25 JUNE 2021

Madam Duval lost her diamond ring
Which to her was a devastating thing
To the police she was quite vocal
She thought their search too **focal**
When they failed to search in Beijing
(She swears it was smuggled in a g-string)

7. EVADE - 26 JUNE 2021

See 169 USHER

Genghis Khan* we madly strove to **evade**
Of his incursions we were afraid
We built cities underground
To avoid being found
And lived there for over a decade
(But got scurvy for lack of lemonade)

8. NAVAL - 27 JUNE 2021

Our battleship numbers are in decline
Pacifists think this is just fine
But if we lose a **naval** battle
Our confidence could rattle
So with our allies we must realign

9. SERVE - 28 JUNE 2021

1

In the infantry Henry did **serve**
While in battle he lost his nerve
He considered desertion
But this required exertion
So he was unable to muster the verve
(Hopefully his mind he'll pre**serve**)

2

While driving drunk the soldier Irv
Came upon a difficult curve
Where the road bended
He was rear ended
He is now unable to **serve**
(He got what he did de**serve**)

10. HEATH - 29 JUNE 2021

The son of Sir Roger Keith
Lived all his life on a **heath**
When old Roger died
His son swooned and cried
For to him a pair of false ivory teeth
(Was the only thing Roger did bequeath)

11. DWARF - 30 JUNE 2021

See 101 SALAD

There once was a giant named Gorf
Who ate walnuts in a salad Waldorf
But the nuts were enchanted
In his pituitary was implanted
A substance that turned him into a **dwarf**
(A mesomorph turned endomorph)*

12. MODEL - 1 JULY 2021

A **model** of fashion design
After a show was forced to resign
Because her bosom was bare
So was her derriere
Yet the critics all thought her divine

13. KARMA - 2 JULY 2021

1
Joe thought meeting Lucy was **karma**
Thus he tried awfully hard to charm her
He thought he was cool
She thought him a fool
It's evident he failed to disarm her

2
In taking a bite of his shawarma
Joel received a dose of **karma**
He insulted the waitress
By calling her tasteless
So she served him eggplant parmigiana

3
A knight in shining armor
Pity he failed to garner
He lost a joust
And later espoused
His failure was due to karma
(Next time he would be a charmer)

14. STINK - 3 JULY 2021

The undies Jill wore were pink
She washed them daily in the sink
When her boyfriend came by
He let out a cry
Now I know why your panties don't **stink**
(She responded with a knowing wink)

15. GRADE - 4 JULY 2021

Our class had to march in a parade
Toiling up a long inclined **grade**
When we reached the hilltop
And the marching could stop
The group flopped down in the shade
(What a great effort we had made)
(Such a performance we displayed!)

16. QUIET - 5 JULY 2021

1
There was an obese fellow named Wyatt
Who needed but avoided a diet
When his wife did admonish
His retort did astonish
He belched then remained completely **quiet**
(Moments later he tried to deny it)

2
All **Quiet** on the Western Front*
Is a novel you must confront
Eric Maria Remarque
In writing it did embark
To depict war's horrors in a tone quite blunt
(Of which he had borne the brunt)

17. BENCH - 6 JULY 2021

While sitting near a lady on a **bench**
I noted a horrible stench
I assumed it was flatulence
Triggered by her petulance
Until it dawned on me that she was drenched

18. ABATE - 7 JULY 2021

See 45 CRATE 110 ABACK

There was an Arab from Kuwait
Who was significantly overweight
Advised a Paleo diet
He refused to try it
His hyperphagia* will never **abate**

His obesity affected his gait
His pupils were unable to dilate
He consulted a neurologist
Was referred to an endocrinologist*
Now the referrals will never **abate**

19. FEIGN - 8 JULY 2021

Joe often **feigned** not feeling well
Once he even pretended he fell
He acted dumb as a mule
To avoid going to school
No one expected he'd win a Nobel

20. MAJOR - 9 JULY 2021

1

As a **major** in the U.S. Air Force
I played poker and bet on a horse
But I'd never win
I became a has-been
Penniless and full of remorse
(Of course)

2

There was something that I did not know
So it came as a **major** blow
Whenever I'd enrage her
I could never assuage her
Now all arguments I try to forgo
(It's either that or find a new beau)

3

There is a baritone from Tennessee
Who never sings in a **major** key
For he can't carry a tune
With a piano or bassoon
Anyone nearby is certain to flee

21. DEATH - 10 JULY 2021

See 369(2) BRINK 382 FLUFF for 21(1)

1

It is said that you will know of your **death**
When you've taken your very last breath
Tomorrow, tomorrow and tomorrow
If you allow me to borrow
From the soliloquy of Shakespeare's Macbeth*

2

When will the Grim Reaper* come for you
Nobody has the slightest clue
When he shows up with Thanatos*
It will be your Alamo*
Death has arrived and you are through
(It can happen if you don't tie your shoe)

22. FRESH - 11 JULY 2021

1

A Pakistani by the name of Koresh
Desired a girl that was **fresh**
So he searched high and low
Found one that looked like Monroe
But regrettably the two didn't mesh
(Perhaps he should look in Bangladesh)

23. CRUST - 12 JULY 2021

The bread was so old that the **crust**
Developed a mold so robust
Yet Fleming* was willin'
To discover penicillin
Not discard it in complete disgust
(Now another one doesn't bite the dust*)

24. STOOL - 13 JULY 2021

A Scatologist* learned while in school
To get information from dinosaur **stool**
First confirm that the sample
Contains scat that is ample
And has not been collected by a fool
(Who on the specimen would drool)

25. COLON - 14 JULY 2021

An anxious man named Nolan
Suffered from an irritable **colon**
Whenever he ate gluten
He couldn't stop tootin'
As he had only a semi**colon**
(The rest of his **colon** was stolen)

26. ABASE - 15 JULY 2021

Behind a woman tying her shoelace
His behavior was an absolute disgrace
When she turned around
His shock was profound
For it was his mother that he did **abase**

27. MARRY - 16 JULY 2021

Barbara was desperate to **marry**
Any Tom Dick or Harry
The chance never arose
No one would propose
So she signed up and joined the military
(Better than a religious seminary)

28. REACT - 17 JULY 2021

1
There was an athlete named Mack
Who ran hard around a racetrack
When he stumbled and fell
Although it hurt like hell
He continued to run and not **react**
(The show must go on if he's intact)

2
It is considered a fact
That women will over**react**
When you are out of place
And insult them to their face
You'd be lucky not to get whacked
(Next time consider a little tact)

29. BATTY - 18 JULY 2021

There once was a woman a fatty
Who hailed from Cincinnati
Who would eat her boogers
Which made her look meshuga*
But she was just inordinately **batty**

30. PRIDE - 19 JULY 2021
See 159(2) WROTE for 30(2)

1
Jill was unable to decide
Whether to run or to hide
When receiving an award
All the attention felt untoward
As she was looked upon with **pride**
(With her family all there at her side)

Pride and Prejudice by Jane Austen*
Is a book that you can get lost in
Elizabeth and Darcy
Eye to eye could not see
But they wed before the towel was tossed in
(I hear they've moved to Boston)

31. FLOSS - 20 JULY 2021

There was a dumb fellow named Ross
Who refused to use dental **floss**
After becoming edentulous*
He was incredulous
He could hardly believe the loss
(Not being able to cuss made him cross)

32. HELIX - 21 JULY 2021

A graduate student named Felix
Studied the DNA **helix**
With Watson and Crick*
Which was quite the trick
Because he majored in orthopedics

33. CROAK - 22 JULY 2021

When uncle Abe was about to **croak**
On his deathbed he softly spoke
You won't find this funny
Don't plan on my money
You see the truth is I'm actually broke
(At this his family started to choke)
(How could they now afford their coke?)

34. STAFF - 23 JULY 2021

A zookeeper while attending a giraffe
Frequently hit it on the legs with a **staff**
Once he hit it on its rump
Causing it to take a dump
Yes the quadruped had the last laugh

35. PAPER - 24 JULY 20

See 1 REBUT for 35(2)

1

I read in yesterday's news**paper**
About a truly intriguing caper
A bank holdup without a gun
Robbers got the job done
By releasing a smoky obscuring vapor
(Sadly all they stole was graph **paper**)

2

Ancient Egyptians knew a thing or two
We've learned from the things they drew
They wrote on papyrus **paper**
Drawing on stone with a scraper
In hieroglyphics* to get through to you
(They had knowledge up the wazoo)

36. UNFED - 25 JULY 2021

Bob was a nasty old dunderhead
Whose long-term grudge remained **unfed**
Against his former boss
Who did a double-cross
Although the cruel fellow was long dead
(I hear he faked it and merely fled)

37. WHELP - 26 JULY 2021
See 90 ROUND

From the pound I rescued a canine **whelp**
Thinking it would give me some help
But the dog was lazy
It would drive me crazy
All he wanted to do was eat kelp
(I'll leave a bad review on Yelp)

38. TRAWL - 27 JULY 2021

A gentleman from Montreal
Through the internet did **trawl**
To find a wife
To be with all his life
But finding her proved his downfall
(Now he hides in the bathroom stall)

39. OUTDO - 28 JULY 2021
See 57 STAND for 39(2)

1

I grew up with a girl named Sue
Whom I always tried to **outdo**
But I couldn't compete
Always suffering defeat
Now she's the one I'm afraid to pursue
(But I don't think she has a clue)

2

Among the tribe the Dakota Sioux*
Your elders you should never **outdo**
To attempt to defeat
Or engage to compete
Is considered extremely taboo
(Unless you want to start a coup)

40. ADOBE - 29 JULY 2021

A determined man named Kobi
Planned to build a home of **adobe***
But was forced to pivot
As no one would visit
He had planned to build it in the Gobi*
(Now he's considering to build in Nairobi)

41. CRAZY - 30 JULY 2021

1

Famous director Martin Scorsese
Considered a film about a daisy
Using slow motion and freeze frame
To be made into a video game
But it's clear the idea was just **crazy**
(I hear he was going to cast Jay Z)

2

Edison thought AC current was **crazy**
Tesla thought DC current was lazy
Their competition grew heated*
And Edison was defeated
But due praise for Tesla was hazy
(Musk's car named Tesla does amaze me)

42. SOWER - 31 JULY 2021

In Dante's* Inferno **sower**s of discord
Earned a special place in hell as their reward
Only one circle lower*
Below the bullshit thrower
Dwelled souls punished by a waterboard
(And the hapless souls who sneezed and snored)

43. REPAY - 1 AUGUST 2021

My best friend who lives in Bombay
Forgot to wish me a happy birthday
This changed my outlook
So by hook or by crook
I will soon find a way to **repay**
(Perhaps time zones had led him astray)

44. DIGIT - 2 AUGUST 2021

There was an innovative midget
Who invented a useless widget
The patent was declined
Which he felt was unkind
So he gave them an upright middle **digit**

45. CRATE - 3 AUGUST 2021

See 18 ABATE 110 ABACK

A trucker who drove interstate*
Had to haul an oversized **crate**
Which fell off his truck
Thanks to bad luck
He's now hiding out in Kuwait
(Where he's learning to roller skate)

46. CLUCK - 4 AUGUST 2021

Frank was a really dumb **cluck**
Who never had any luck
When he won the lottery
It was clear for all to see
He had transformed into a lucky schmuck*
(Now he can afford a pet duck)

47. SPIKE - 5 AUGUST 2021

1

General Eisenhower's nickname was Ike*
He led the battle against the third Reich
When he became POTUS*
Americans failed to notice
The absence of an unemployment **spike**
(And the lack of a labor union strike)

2

A sneaky fellow by the name of Mike
His date's drink he did love to spike
For when inebriated
Her concerns were abated
She was less likely to say go take a hike
(He needs an evaluation by psych)

48. MIMIC - 6 AUGUST 2021

Once a violent bruiser I did **mimic**
But he was not a fan of my gimmick
He punched me in the nose
With two terrific blows
Now you'll find me at a local walk-in clinic

49. POUND - 7 AUGUST 2021

See 90 ROUND for 49(2)

1

Britain traded the euro for the **pound**
A decision thought to be profound
When they left the EU*
They told Europe to go screw
Not everyone thought Brexit* was sound

They are so gorgeously round
Forming a perfect mound
With a nipple of a navel*
Your taste buds they'll enable
Oranges two dollars to the **pound**
(Ha ha I had you all wound)

50. MAXIM - 8 AUGUST 2021

Actions speak louder than words
Is a **maxim** everyone has heard
But it is not always true
For out of the blue
Reality proves this absurd

51. LINEN - 9 AUGUST 2021

See 216 PRICK

A colonial spinster* named McKinnon
On a wheel was always spinnin'
She was in high demand
For she had a gifted hand
In creating the most beautiful **linen**
(But knock after hours and catch her sinnin')
(Which was in higher demand I can't put a pin in*)

52. UNMET - 10 AUGUST 2021

He was her best lover yet
But her needs remain **unmet**
For she has a compulsion
That causes a convulsion
Which her lovers can never forget
(Don't ask about the clarinet)

53. FLESH - 11 AUGUST 2021

There was a hungry man named Blake
Who longed for a Wagyu steak
But at his butcher the **flesh**
Did not look very fresh
So he decided to bake a cake
(Now he's got a tummy ache)

54. BOOBY - 12 AUGUST 2021

See 271(1) MOVIE for 54(2)

1

There was an ignorant chap
Who stepped on a **booby** trap
There was no explosion
While he was in motion
So he decided to take a nap
(He awoke screaming Holy Crap!)

2

Jack promised to give Jill a ruby
If she allowed him to feel her **booby**
When she said it's alright
He squeezed with all his might
Now she's sorry she accepted a newbie
(Who's next I wonder could you be)

55. FORTH - 13 AUGUST 2021

An explorer whose name was Roth
Tried to reach the farthest longitude north
By the time he reached the pole
He had lost complete control
To go more north he could no longer go **forth**
(He did meet Santa Claus for what it's worth)

56. FIRST - 14 AUGUST 2021

The media empire of William Randolph Hurst*
Was certainly known as America's **first**
When Welles made Citizen Kane*
It drove old Hurst insane
So on this film he placed a dreadful curse
(For my ticket I want to be reimbursed)

57. STAND - 15 AUGUST 2021

See 39(2) OUTDO

It's not very difficult to under**stand**
Why the battle didn't go as planned
Sitting Bull was a smart
Sioux warrior with heart
At Little Bighorn or Custer's last **stand***

58. BELLY - 16 AUGUST 2021

See 103 SPICY

A dear friend of mine from New Delhi
Had breath that was always smelly
For he ate so much food
Indian spices he'd exude
And developed a rotund pot **belly**

59. IVORY - 17 AUGUST 2021

1
A man from the **Ivory** Coast
Adored eating jam on toast
When his toaster died
He wept and he cried
In its memory he remained engrossed
(Now he will reluctantly eat pot roast)

2
Piano keys were once made of **ivory***
Now only obtainable by thievery
For the tusk of an elephant
To the animal is more relevant
Not hunting them seems very wise to me
(There are better options for finery)

60. SEEDY - 18 AUGUST 2021

There was an old man who was greedy
His eyes were small and rather beady
He hated to clean
Even his latrine
Consequently his house was quite **seedy**
(Anyone visiting made their exit speedy)

61. PRINT - 19 AUGUST 2021

1
A counterfeiter by the name of Clint
Failed to imitate the US Mint
He tried to **print** money
With the help of his honey
Both are now serving a long jail stint

2
I desired to own a Gustav Klimt*
But could only afford a **print**
Oh his painting The Kiss
Is impossible to resist
To understand it one needs to squint
(Can you see it or do you need a hint)

62. YEARN - 20 AUGUST 2021

1

A vivacious lady named Fern
When young I did hastily spurn
Twenty years later
She's a legislator
Now it is my turn to **yearn**
(I'll wait for my heart to adjourn)

2

There was a sweet lady named Fern
For whom I did desperately **yearn**
Not just for her beauty
Or her sense of duty
It was for the tricks she could turn
(I wonder how much does she earn)

63. DRAIN - 21 AUGUST 2021

1

In Chile I have heard some scientists claim
Water goes counterclockwise down a **drain***
Yet north of the equator
Many a navigator
Believe that this a fictitious refrain
(The Coriolis effect is to blame)

2

While climbing up a rocky terrain
My sinuses began to **drain**
I was unable yodel
Now this is anecdotal
My snot was quite hard to contain
(Fats would say ain't that a shame*)

64. BRIBE - 22 AUGUST 2021

As a member of the Pawnee tribe
I naturally love to imbibe
Yet being intoxicated
Is highly overrated
It makes you vulnerable to taking a **bribe**
(Next time I'll only offer hygrocybe*)

65. STOUT - 23 AUGUST 2021

Stuart is rather **stout**
Of this there is little doubt
One day a severe pain
In his big toe did sustain
Clearly he has gotten the gout

Stuart has a **stout** heart
Evident right from the start
But he is terribly savage
After eating stuffed cabbage
That's when he's unable to control a fart
(Eating near him is not so smart)

66. PANEL - 24 AUGUST 2021
See 201 BANAL

As a member of the jury **panel**
I wasn't allowed to wear flannel
A jacket and necktie
I had to abide by
Now don't you consider that banal

67. CRASS - 25 AUGUST 2021

There was once an irascible lass
Who in public would scratch her ass
Accused of being lewd
She replied that's misconstrued
I'm not vulgar but I'm certainly **crass**
(Now don't give me no sass)

68. FLUME - 26 AUGUST 2021

A forty-niner who went by the name of Bloom
While prospecting for gold dug a **flume***
But the river nearby
During a drought ran dry
So he never experienced the boom
(This cast him into a massive gloom)
(It got better when he became a groom)

69. OFFAL - 27 AUGUST 2021

There was an impoverished Czech
Who considered **offal*** to be dreck*
On the verge of starvation
It was his salvation
So he ate it and said what the heck
(Now he eats every speck)

70. AGREE - 28 AUGUST 2021

A snobbish British Marquis
With his fiancé could never **agree**
She was an American
They argued over and again
Whether to drink coffee or tea

71. ERROR - 29 AUGUST 2021

Perhaps it was simply an **error**
But his prank resulted in terror
He snuck up on his sister
Passionately kissed her
Which shocked and really did scare her
(With a therapist she now does confer)

72. SWIRL - 30 AUGUST 2021

There was a young lass named Merle
Who loved to eat soft ice cream **swirl**
The truth was such
That she ate too much
Which caused her to heave and to hurl
(Especially after too many a twirl)

73. ARGUE - 31 AUGUST 2021

1
A crooked lawyer is always on cue
To rebut and to **argue**
Only truth is of import
With any legal case in court
Then he'll turn around and overcharge you
(And move onto the next in queue)

2
A gay man who lived in Khartoum*
Took a lesbian up to his room
And they **argue**d all night
Over who had the right
To do what and with which and to whom

74. BLEED - 1 SEPTEMBER 2021

See 180 USING

He suffered from Hemophilia B*
Tsar Nicholas' son Alexei*
When the lad began to **bleed**
Who was called in with speed
Rasputin* the mad monk expediently
(He's using the tsarevich for his power spree)
(He needs to shape his beard into a goatee)

75. DELTA - 2 SEPTEMBER 2021

1

On a riverboat in the Mississippi **delta**
Sue didn't like the poker hand dealt her
When another gambler's wife
Pulled out a Bowie knife
Everything quickly went helter-skelter

2

At college a differential equation
Was to me a thing of fascination
How did the **delta** symbol*
Make calculations nimble
For mathematicians of every nation
(Just don't ask me for a citation)

76. FLICK - 3 SEPTEMBER 2021

1

It was gelatinous and thick
Obtained with a finger pick
She pulled it from her nose
But didn't wipe it on her clothes
She merely gave it a vigorous **flick**
(Isn't she one heck of a chick)

2
His name was Dirty Dick
And Sally was his chick
They were quite a pair
That everyone did fear
Characters in a crime **flick**
(Until she left him for Nick)
(Now he needs a new schtick)

77. TOTEM - 4 SEPTEMBER 2021

1
The Norse god of war Odin*
Is frequently used as a **totem**
If worn in battle
Your nerves will never rattle
Unless you are under an evil omen
(If so better keep roamin')

2
The porcupine once was his **totem**
But this prickly emblem smote him
Carrying it in his underpants
Performing a native dance
Severely disfigured his scrotum
(Now it hurts to tote 'em)

78. WOOER - 5 SEPTEMBER 2021

When young she had many a **wooer**
As she aged there were fewer and fewer
As an old maid
She became dismayed
As nobody cared to pursue her
(Now she wants something to renew her)
(Maybe some potion you can brew her)

79. FRONT - 6 SEPTEMBER 2021

1
It was difficult to disguise
For in **front** of my eyes
A man took a dump
A steamy smelly lump
In Los Angeles no surprise

2
My business is really a **front**
Police attention it does shunt
My dance of confusion
Is an act of diffusion
So detection we'll never have to confront
(Its prostitution to be blunt)

80. SHRUB - 7 SEPTEMBER 2021

A **shrub** is a plant without a trunk
A place that could hide a skunk
A chipmunk and a hare
But it couldn't hide a bear
Unless the poor grizzly was drunk
(That might be a myth to debunk)

81. PARRY - 8 SEPTEMBER 2021

Gertrude summarily wanted to marry
A world-renowned fencer named Harry
So she repeatedly did thrust
In his face her massive bust
Yet somehow he managed to **parry**
(Before the situation got rather hairy)

82. BIOME - 9 SEPTEMBER 2021

Everyone has a **biome**
Microbes making their home
In our intestine
Which they rest in
Saving us from irritable bowel syndrome
(Giving you freedom to roam)

83. LAPEL - 10 SEPTEMBER 2021
See 257(2) MOURN

He wore a carnation in his **lapel**
For he thought that it looked swell
Then he traveled by car
To a place above the bar
His absolutely favorite brothel
(They make a great waffle)

84. START - 11 SEPTEMBER 2021
See 158 RETCH for 84(1)

1

I don't know how to **start**
My sad story from the heart
While we were copulating
It was so irritating
Our love died with her awful fart
(Nothing else could have torn us apart)

2

I wonder could we **start** again
I don't know where or when
You really broke my heart
When you decided we would part
Yet for you I still have such a yen
(Meet you at the bullpen?)

85. GREET - 12 SEPTEMBER 2021

1
Every time that we happen to meet
I'm uncertain just how to **greet**
For I feel a twinge of guilt
Boy she is really built
The gal with whom once I did cheat
(Getting away with it has been a feat)
(Not an action I'll likely repeat)

2
At our very first and only meeting
I was unsure of the proper **greet**ing
How does one address the king
So I never said a thing
I simply bowed and began retreating

86. GONER - 13 SEPTEMBER 2021

When it's hopeless and you are a **goner**
It would certainly be a great honor
To lie perfectly still
So formaldehyde won't spill
For Mr O'Conner your expert embalmer
(He's the one to make you eternally calmer)

87. GOLEM - 14 SEPTEMBER 2021
See 3 HUMPH

Last year I raced in a slalom*
Against a creature called the **Golem***
Too clumsy to zig zag
Or ski inside the flags
He could only ski in a straight column
(Now the poor thing is rather solemn)

88. LUSTY - 15 SEPTEMBER 2021

She was so strong and **lusty**
Also impressively busty
I became fearful you see
When she said sleep with me
As I was too old and rusty

She was so young and **lusty**
While I was old and crusty
Unable to please her
Having no wish to tease her
I named her my will's trustee
(The easiest route you'll agree)

89. LOOPY - 16 SEPTEMBER 2021

1
A Japanese man Suzuki
Desired to play kabuki*
It is sad but a fact
He was unable to act
As his behavior was completely **loopy**
(His wife was his only groupie)

2
A raunchy woman named Lupe
Exhibited behavior absurdly **loopy**
For she desired to sleep
With three men and two sheep
And to yell out loud and to cheer "whoopee"
(All of this made her husband droopy)

90. ROUND - 17 SEPTEMBER 2021
See 37 WHELP

It was an awful growling sound
Going **round** and **round**
Producing haunting chills
The Hound of the Baskervilles*
A dog hellbent for the pound

91. AUDIT - 18 SEPTEMBER 2021

No citizen could ever applaud it
A damn IRS **audit**
By the time agents go away
The amount you'll have to pay
Will leave you feeling ramrodded
(Not only that but poked and prodded)

92. LYING - 19 SEPTEMBER 2021

I knew that she was **lying**
Her story I wasn't buying
Our marriage was in peril
Due to her affair with Cheryl
So much for love being undying

93. GAMMA - 20 SEPTEMBER 2021
See 277(1) PURGE for 93(1)
See 160(1) CLOCK 179(1) TRACE for 93(2)

1
This may not be proper grammar
But I'm third in line or **gamma***
I'm a chimpanzee
Who waits patiently
For a deliciously ripe banana
(Hard to find here in the savanna)

2
I simply do not know what to say
After being struck by a **gamma** ray*
While exploring outer space
I must be replaced
For very soon I will start to decay
(All of me except my toupee)

94. LABOR - 21 SEPTEMBER 2021

1
A good Samaritan named Graber
Heard awful screaming by his neighbor
When he rushed to assist
She did not resist
As she was in the late stage of **labor**

2
A Frenchman by the name of Lefebre
Murdered his poor wife with a saber
Found guilty by the jury
He now resides in Missouri
Serving 20 years hard **labor**
(Too bad he didn't use a tabor*)

95. ISLET - 22 SEPTEMBER 2021

There are **islet**s of Langerhans*
Throughout our pancreatic glands
That make glucagon and insulin
So you can eat sugar and stay thin
But don't let the sweets get out of hand
(Ignore the many in my mouth crammed)

96. CIVIC - 23 SEPTEMBER 2021

In the big apple a mayor named Rudy*
Thought it was his **civic** duty
To control rampant crime
Surging at that time
Reducing it to less than in Djibouti
(Not to mention he was a cutie)

97. FORGE - 24 SEPTEMBER 2021

1

The British were unable to disgorge
The continental army from Valley **Forge***
During 6 months of that year
American soldiers bivouacked there
Under the leadership of General George
(The mosquitoes there were a scourge)

2

She **forged** the dang document
Without my knowledge or consent
During our tumultuous divorce
A restraining order was in force
So much discord did she foment*
(She caused my squash to ferment)

98. CORNY - 25 SEPTEMBER 2021

1

The issue was rather thorny
Presenting a problem for me
When she scoffed at my joke
I might have misspoke
When I used schmaltzy* instead of **corny**
(Time to call up my attorney)

2
There was a young gal named Sigourney
Who claimed she did adore me
I responded Oy Vey*
Such a strange thing to say
She got livid as my response was so **corny**
(Since that day I have been rather horny)

99. MOULT - 26 SEPTEMBER 2021

See 315 LARVA for 99(2)

1
What a sudden unexpected jolt
Causing me to want to revolt
It's terribly unfair
I'm losing my hair
And not undergoing a **moult***

2
What an unanticipated jolt
When I observed a huge snake **moult**
I will tell no lies
It took me by surprise
So I ran like a thunderbolt
(Now inside I use my deadbolt)

100. BASIC - 27 SEPTEMBER 2021

1
I was on a lifelong search
Even did **basic** lab research
To find the meaning of life
And the cause of so much strife
Now I'm back to praying in church

2
When recruited into the army
Mother worried it would harm me
I had no way of explaining
That during **basic** training
No need to send a kosher salami
(Although it does have that umami)

101. SALAD - 28 SEPTEMBER 2021

See 11 DWARF

There once was a duck a mallard
Born looking rather pallid
He thought he was camouflaged
Until a hunter he failed to dodge
And wound up in a Caesar **salad**
(To this day they sing a ballad)

102. AGATE - 29 SEPTEMBER 2021

A dishonest fellow named Schwartz
Loved **agate** a form of quartz
So he stole a supply
An act he did deny
No one now believes a thing he purports
(As you can imagine he's now out of sorts)

103. SPICY - 30 SEPTEMBER 2021

See 58 BELLY

1
In bed she was cold and icy
Although she was rather pricey
For as a professional
She was unexceptional
But with her lover she was terribly **spicy**
(Why she gets hired is dicey)

2

I love Indian food's flavor
Every **spicy** speck to savor
But effects on my bowel
Make me cramp and howl
The details I will waiver
(Believe me I'm doing you a favor)

104. SPRAY - 1 OCTOBER 2021

It's a painful story to convey
I once used a woman's hair **spray**
Which came in a can
That said not for a man
Since that day my hair is completely gray
(Since then I've been completely gay)
(But I might have always been that way)
(Who can really say)

105. ESSAY - 2 OCTOBER 2021

In college I wrote an **essay**
On thoughts I wished to convey
But I was graded a D
Which forced me to see
I'd be better off studying ballet
(I do well shaking my bootay)

106. FJORD - 3 OCTOBER 2021

I thought I never could afford
To cruise a Norwegian **fjord**
But luck did stun
Native Dancer* won
Now I will be on board
(I shot and I scored)

107. SPEND - 4 OCTOBER 2021

1
I finally reached a dead end
Compulsively I did **spend**
With the market crash
I ran out of cash
Now I live off my girlfriend
(On her I so strongly depend)
(I'd better never offend)

2
I can't believe all the time I did **spend**
On what proved to be a dead end
Reading books I abhor
Most a dreadful bore
On the recommendation of a friend

108. KEBAB - 5 OCTOBER 2021

I once thought he was a heartthrob
Until I saw him eating shish **kebab**
Biting down he did drool
He looked like a fool
Now I realize he was always a slob
(Don't watch him eat corn on the cob)

109. GUILD - 6 OCTOBER 2021

1
In the Middle Ages to join a **guild**
You needed to be competent and skilled
But if you were a Jew*
You'd be told to go screw
As money lender you would have to feel fulfilled

2
As a member of a theatrical **guild**
I was feeling somewhat unfulfilled
Yet I was not leaning
Towards up and leaving
Until for membership I was finally billed

110. ABACK - 7 OCTOBER 2021

See 18 ABATE 45 CRATE

I was quite taken **aback**
By the intensity of the attack
Saddam invaded Kuwait
Coalition forces did liberate
With a shock and awe counterattack*
(What happens when you talk smack*)

111. MOTOR - 8 OCTOBER 2021

1
Deep in your **motor** cortex
You always cogitate on sex
Every moment it seems
Even in your dreams
In your mind it's always in context
(Don't forget to wear your Gore-Tex*)

2
A trumpeter by the name of Schroeder
To his horn attached a **motor**
To remotely play valves
Free to boost morales
And play a round of strip poker
(That's what made his performance mediocre)

112. ALONE - 9 OCTOBER 2021

1

A tone-deaf musician named Leone
Decided to play the trombone
Whenever he'd play
His audience ran away
Now he's forced to play all **alone**
(Someone throw this poor guy a bone)

2

There was a dapper seducer Ramon
Who employed a malodorous cologne
But couldn't understand
He should change his brand
As he did all his courting by telephone
(Eventually he wound up **alone**)

113. HATCH - 10 OCTOBER 2021

A complex plot I once did **hatch**
For my wife to finally catch
In flagrante delicto*
Or under mistletoe
But she was simply grooming her snatch
(Her underwear she did dispatch)

114. HYPER - 11 OCTOBER 2021

In Hamelin lived the Pied Piper*
Known to be really **hyper**
It was such a pity
Rats overran his city
Now he's become a cipher
(He should have become a rat sniper)

115. THUMB - 12 OCTOBER 2021

1
On my journey I tried and tried
Desperately to **thumb** a ride
This was never to be
For it's plain to see
No boats ever came in with the tide
(On this island I'm forced to reside)

2
There once was a homeless bum
At opulence his nose would **thumb**
But upon acquiring wealth
By prevarication and stealth
He realized that was really dumb
(To this way of life he did succumb)

3
Tom **Thumb*** whom children adore
Is a small person of English Folklore
Although he was small
Adventures tested his gall
And from his matchbox bed he would snore

116. DOWRY - 13 OCTOBER 2021

An ambitious fellow named Lowery
Proposed to a gal with face flowery
He cared not for her beauty
Nor her strong sense of duty
But only for her rather large **dowry**
(Learning this turned her sour-y)

117. OUGHT - 14 OCTOBER 2021

Prince Charles recently claimed the British throne
During his lifetime he **ought** to have known
Before rising so high
Queen Liz would have to die
As long as she was never overthrown
(Unless she was replaced by a clone)

118. BELCH - 15 OCTOBER 2021

A flatulent fellow named Welch
Loud farts was unable to squelch
When eventually he could
He finally understood
It was more socially accepted to **belch**

119. DUTCH - 16 OCTOBER 2021

1
A cheapskate by the name of Nate
To women was unable to relate
When he asked a gal out
Success was in doubt
For he always offered to **Dutch** date*

2
The people whom we call the **Dutch**
Do not refer to themselves as such
They prefer Nederlanders*
As they don't come from Flanders
To remember this won't take that much

120. PILOT - 17 OCTOBER 2021

I once had to **pilot** a plane
Through a tropical hurricane
All aboard did survive
A prolonged steep nosedive
Not ejecting was considered insane

121. TWEED - 18 OCTOBER 2021

1
A crooked politician Boss **Tweed***
In embezzling millions did succeed
But justice prevailed
When he was jailed
He escaped was recaptured then never freed
(To pneumonia he did finally concede)

2
A stoner professor always wore **tweed**
With dinner he loved to drink mead
When he taught biology
And lectured psychology
He always prepared by smoking weed

122. COMET - 19 OCTOBER 2021
See 290 NATAL

Halley's **comet** comes every seventy four years
Its arrival creates irrational fears
But for author Mark Twain*
It's perihelion once again
Announces his birth and when he disappears
(Doesn't this bring you to tears)

123. JAUNT - 20 OCTOBER 2021

During our leisurely mountain **jaunt**
My wife decided to annoy and taunt
The hell out of me
She was so creepy
I returned looking rather gaunt
(Punishment for eating her croissant)

124. ENEMA - 21 OCTOBER 2021

A sensual woman named Emma
Enjoyed a frequent **enema**
She was never constipated
But they made her feel elated
Now isn't that quite a dilemma

125. STEED - 22 OCTOBER 2021

Sir Gawain rode a trusty **steed**
Which ran with incredible speed
But when Gawain's* armor rusted
The gallant horse was busted
For on his master's armor it had peed

126. ABYSS - 23 OCTOBER 2021

I was falling into a bottomless **abyss**
In an apparent state of bliss
I thought it an earthquake
Till I was forced to awake
By an overwhelming urge to take a piss
(Going back to sleep nothing was amiss)

127. GROWL - 24 OCTOBER 2021

1

I heard a long rumbling **growl**
Emanating from my noisy bowel
Followed by much gas
Exiting my ass
With an odor that was floridly foul
(A perfect description of a fart you'll allow)

2

The beautiful Great Horned Owl
At night will hoot but never howl
While the deadly mountain lion
Especially the Paraguayan
Will fiercely **growl** and scowl
(If he's on the prowl throw in the towel)

128. FLING - 25 OCTOBER 2021

See 164(2) BRING 285 LOWLY

She was certain this was the real thing
Expecting to receive an engagement ring
He was so debonair
But did he really care
Or was this just his usual **fling**
(To him tightly she will cling)
(As his purse has many a loose string)

129. DOZEN - 26 OCTOBER 2021

1

They recruited murderers on death row
To assassinate Nazis at a French chateau
In the movie The Dirty **Dozen***
About which everyone was buzzin'
Not a football but handgrenade did Jim Brown throw

2
A **dozen** is a grouping of twelve
Where that started we can delve
An early integer grouping
Of eggs and the moon including
With only ten digits it's not applied to ourselve
(Perhaps this particular rhyme I should shelve)

130. BOOZY - 27 OCTOBER 2021

1
A refined woman was extremely choosy
About the alcohol she used to feel **boozy**
Preferring single malt scotch
Which she poured on her crotch
For deep down she really was a floozy
(How she cleaned up after was really a doozy)

2
An unfortunate woman named Suzy
Became inordinately **boozy**
Later she was found
Tragically drowned
Inebriated while soaking in her jacuzzi
(Get out if you start to feel woozy)

131. ERODE - 28 OCTOBER 2021

At its end the universe may explode
Alternatively it could implode
But until it comes to an end
Entropy* remains its friend
Causing it to gradually **erode**

132. WORLD - 29 OCTOBER 2021

1

Our **world** is 6000 years old
At least that's what we've been told
But the biblical apostles
Knew nothing of fossils
Something they never did behold
(Perhaps because God never told)

2

The planet we call our **world**
For 4.5 billion years has whirled
On its axis rotating
Continents gyrating
And over time has never unfurled
(We never notice how we are being twirled)

133. GOUGE - 30 OCTOBER 2021

Odysseus never had to **gouge** out an eye
For the Cyclops' meal plan to go awry*
He used a flaming torch
The giant's only eye to scorch
Thus ensuring the brutal beast would die
(And afterwards made a delicious pie)

134. CLICK - 31 OCTOBER 2021

1

Seig Heil when a Nazi salutes
Requires one to **click** their boots
Out of respect for Adolf
Who couldn't play golf
For he was truly a despicable brute

2
We never did **click** as friends
Our views could not make amends
But we were great in bed together
In all kinds of weather
So I hate for us to come to an end
(Let's keep entangling our odds and ends)

135. BRIAR - 1 NOVEMBER 2021

Brer Rabbit* lived in the **briar** patch
While stuck to Tar Baby Brer Fox did snatch
He was such a clever hare
Telling Fox throw me in there
And escaped without even a scratch

136. GREAT - 2 NOVEMBER 2021

See 163 PROVE 187(2) GRIPE for 136(2)

1
For the record I will state
That my woman is really **great**
For she is able to control
Me when I'm an asshole
And my ego to fully deflate*
(And even at times berate)
(But only when I'm in a state)

2
In the 20th century a few men were **great**
Of these few I can certainly state
Churchill Reagan Einstein Freud
Names we should never avoid
Their importance is impossible to overstate

137. ALTAR - 3 NOVEMBER 2021

The one thing in my life I would alter
Is meeting my wife at the **altar**
To join in holy matrimony
Clearly a bunch of baloney
Now I wish I'd allowed myself to f**alter**

138. PULPY - 4 NOVEMBER 2021

1

At the gym I met a gal quite hulky
Her body was muscular and bulky
I frequently fantasized
About touching her thighs
When I did they felt rather **pulpy**
(My disappointment made me quite sulky)

2

I love to drink **pulpy** orange juice
But acid reflux it does induce
So I switched to drinking whisky
Which makes me feel quite frisky
At least that's what I use as an excuse

139. BLURT - 5 NOVEMBER 2021

Our pastor loves to **blurt** out
In sermons that he is so devout
He drinks too much red wine
Upon insistence of the divine
Now he suffers from tophaceous gout
(Yet this never causes him to doubt)

140. COAST - 6 NOVEMBER 2021

Hernando loved to loudly boast
That he was known from **coast** to **coast**
For his jambalaya
A culinary messiah
Until his schizophrenia was diagnosed
(At which point he was properly dosed)
(Now all he makes is jam and toast)

141. DUCHY - 7 NOVEMBER 2021
See 289 SHAWL

Duke William was very touchy
About the size of his **duchy**
Upon exploring its boundaries
He learned with profound unease
They were either too slushy or brushy

Prince William is the Duke of Cornwall
His **duchy** is known to one and to all
Founded in the 14th century
By King Edward the three
It will endure until the monarchy does fall
(This property not intended for use by all)
(When visiting be sure to bring a shawl)

142. GROIN - 8 NOVEMBER 2021

An ignorant man from Des Moines
Developed a swelling in his **groin**
Examined by a lady doctor
He hauled off and socked her
So she prescribed a dose of phenytoin*
(This helped with nothing but losing coin)

143. FIXER - 9 NOVEMBER 2021

He took his girlfriend to a mixer
And gave her an alcoholic elixir
She got carried away
Bawdry behavior on display
Now they need a relationship **fixer**
(All will be well when he licks her)

144. GROUP - 10 NOVEMBER 2021
See 339 ALBUM for 144(1)

1

My favorite singing **group**
Is that wonderful British troop
The Beatles their name
Enjoyed worldwide fame
Upon them smitten young ladies did swoop

2

We indulged in frequent **group** sex
Treating random partners as objects
Oh we had loads of fun
But I'm loath to tell anyone
My wife is unfortunately my Ex

145. ROGUE - 11 NOVEMBER 2021

Eleven died in the Matawan **rogue** shark attack*
To the year 1916 this will take you back
Inspiring the movie Jaws
Sharks were on earth before dinosaurs
This awful event took the world aback
(Imagine encountering the shark's plaque)
(I've heard we make for a good snack)

146. BADLY - 12 NOVEMBER 2021

I told Jill I loved her madly
But she treated me very **badly**
So I courted her sister Louise
But she was a cock tease
Now I'm dating their brother Bradley

147. SMART - 13 NOVEMBER 2021

1

Philosopher Rene Descartes*
Was incredibly **smart**
He thought the seat of the soul
Was the pineal gland's role
Today that theory is picked apart
(Try not to take it to heart)

2

Teddy was a real **smart** ass
A member of the upper class
He flunked out of school
Being dumb as a mule
Not a single course could he pass
(Nowadays he works selling gas)

148. PITHY - 14 NOVEMBER 2021

See 326 FARCE

I once wrote a **pithy** review
On The Taming of the Shrew
That version was unique
I espoused in my critique
For its lead was a kangaroo
(It turned out to be one heck of a debut)

149. GAUDY - 15 NOVEMBER 2021

My childhood girlfriend Maudie
Loved to wear clothes quite **gaudy**
But as the years passed
Style she has amassed
Now she dresses in a manner haughty
(Especially when she's being naughty)
(It pays to be fabulously bawdy)

150. CHILL - 16 NOVEMBER 2021

1

Her voice was high pitched and shrill
Which produced in me quite a **chill**
At her singing premier
The boos were severe
Now I've heard she's retired to Brazil
(Though she still sings the Barber of Seville*)

2

I was told I had better **chill** out
When suddenly I began to shout
After taking LSD
Everyone would agree
What was real was seriously in doubt
(Help am I drowning in sauerkraut)

151. HERON - 17 NOVEMBER 2021
See 378 Egret

An eccentric lady named Erin
Owned a beautiful pet **heron**
She became dismayed
When before her laid
Her poor bird cooked in a terrine*

I often seem to forget
A **heron** is not an egret
The French are one of the few
That cook either in a stew
The distinction they never do fret
(Referring to either as a poulette*)

152. VODKA - 18 NOVEMBER 2021

I just learned that my family doctor
Was a star of college soccer
Now he's unable to play
For over time he did stray
By becoming addicted to **vodka**

153. FINER - 19 NOVEMBER 2021

I told a gal nothing could be **finer**
Than to closely inspect her vagina
She replied that's likely true
Then she wound up and threw
A punch that gave me a big shiner
(Should have tried to wine and dine her)

154. SURER - 20 NOVEMBER 2021

I most certainly did adore her
Of that I could never be **surer**
She was a skydiver
An extreme sports survivor
Lloyds of London refused to insure her
(I don't think it's possible to restore her)

155. RADIO - 21 NOVEMBER 2021

1

His short-wave signals traversed the Atlantic
An important advance not just pedantic
Who invented **radio**
Italian Marconi Guglielmo?*
Tesla's claim of the patent was not just semantic

2

A singer named Fazio
Listened only to **radio**
The tenor was blind
But he didn't mind
He had no interest in video
(As long as he could sing an arpeggio)

156. ROUGE - 22 NOVEMBER 2021

Rouge is made of rust*
For an actress it's a must
Should she lack a gentle touch
She could apply too much
And appear to have a menopausal flush
(Imbuing in others disgust)

157. PERCH - 23 NOVEMBER 2021

1

A pigeon roosted inside a church
Using the spire as a **perch**
With worshipers in the pew
It did what birds do
The congregants it did besmirch
(Causing many a stomach to lurch)

2
There has not been any research
On why the freshwater **perch**
Is used in gefilte fish
A tasty Jewish dish
Rarely ever served in a church
(For many hours I did search)

158. RETCH - 24 NOVEMBER 2021
See 84(1) START

I imagine you will think I'm a kvetch*
But the smell of farts makes me **retch**
It's the hydrogen sulfide*
I'm unable to abide
In my olfactory memory it is etched

159. WROTE - 25 NOVEMBER 2021
See 30(2) PRIDE

1
I try very hard not to gloat
Critics assume what I **wrote**
Is to be taken seriously
When my intent is hilarity
My goal is my name to promote
(I just think I'm the GOAT*)

2
Who's the one author of any who **wrote**
That others most frequently quote
Oscar Wilde* for humorous
Jane Austen most numerous
In second place Shakespeare likely receives your vote
(Though about this I doubt he does gloat)

160. CLOCK - 26 NOVEMBER 2021

See 93(2) GAMMA 179(1) TRACE

1

A **clock** marks the passage of time
Yet an error can occur along the line
Vibrating quartz crystals electronic
Make a ticking **clock** atomic
Providing accurate spacetime* sublime
(It will never change on a dime)

2

Hickory dickory dock
A mouse ran up the **clock**
In this nursery rhyme
The **clock** won't chime
For its movement the mouse did block

161. TILDE - 27 NOVEMBER 2021

1

A Spanish author named Matilda
With the 'N' never used a **tilde***
Her prose was not good
She was misunderstood
She stopped writing and became a builder

2

Aboard ship the use of a gimbal*
Makes accurate navigation nimble
Never use a **tilde**
In a naval flotilla
For it is an approximation symbol*

162. STORE - 28 NOVEMBER 2021

1
When I signed up for the Marine Corps
I had no idea what was in **store**
Now Semper Fi*
I'm willing to die
I'm always ready to go to war

2
The Norse god of war
Goes by the name of Thor*
When he goes into battle
He makes quite a rattle
Pulling his hammer from the armory **store**
(Pray with you he doesn't need to settle a score)

163. PROVE - 29 NOVEMBER 2021
See 136(2) GREAT

On Einstein one never could im**prove**
Abstract thinking was his groove
Deducing $E=mc^2$*
Was not just hot air
And certainly quite difficult to **prove**
(Of this and his mustache we ap**prove**)

164. BRING - 30 NOVEMBER 2021
See 128 FLING 236 PAUSE 285 LOWLY

Although it is a juvenile thing
To Christmas Eve I continue to cling
As an adult
I still exult
The wonder of what Santa will **bring**

One year he did **bring** a strange thing
Not knowing what to do with a G-string
I decided to wear it
Being careful not to tear it
And had myself one hell of a fling

165. SOLVE - 1 DECEMBER 2021

1

The killer's identity remained unknown
So the police brought in Sherlock Holmes
They were unable to **solve**
How the crime did evolve
But they knew he'd leave no unturned stone
(Cocaine does put him in the zone)

2

The greatest number of detective mysteries
Was written by Dame Agatha Christie*
Hercule Poirot went sniffing
When Agatha went missing*
But all the evidence proved contradictory
(I'm still waiting on this piece of history)

166. CHEAT - 2 DECEMBER 2021

See 168 EXULT 394(2) FLOCK for 166(1)

1

Satan will use every type of deceit
Pretending that he won't **cheat**
So you'll sell your soul*
Signing his scroll
When you die you're going to feel the heat

2
Your **Cheat**in' Heart was written and recorded
By singer Hank Williams it was reported
At thirty he's deceased
Shortly after the song's released
Not enough time for accolades to be awarded

For his untimely death he had himself to blame
He became an alcoholic oh dear what a shame
George Hamilton was groovy
Playing him in a movie*
In which Hank Williams Jr sang to great acclaim
(All the **cheat**in' drove poor Hank insane)

167. GRIME - 3 DECEMBER 2021

1
The bayou was filled with primordial slime
And I was completely covered in **grime**
With an alligator hunting guide
We hiked to where they reside
Now I'm too frightened to continue this rhyme

2
What in the heck is **grime** music
It certainly is not therapeutic
A mix of hip hop rap and techno
Do I want to hear it heck no
I am certain it will make me feel sick
(Some classical music will do the trick)

168. EXULT - 4 DECEMBER 2021

See 166(1) CHEAT 394(2) FLOCK

I once considered joining a cult
Heard it was Satan they did **exult**
But I changed my mind
And ultimately declined
For I never believed in the occult
(Turns out I'm a responsible adult)

169. USHER - 5 DECEMBER 2021

See 7 EVADE 317(1) STORY 380(1) SEVER for 169(1)

1

The Fall of The House of **Usher*** you know
Was written by the great Edgar Allan Poe
The story is quite macabre
It would make a good opera
Although the libretto might be a bit slow

I was **usher**ed down a hall
Leading to a wine cellar wall
Enticed with a trick
Entombed in a wall of brick
Toward death I now irretrievably fall
(Without Amontillado* or even a shawl)

2

We were **usher**ed down a hall
Which led us to a big wall
After many an erratic turn
How were we to return
From the underground city of Montreal*
(Where I come from I can't now recall)

170. EPOCH - 6 DECEMBER 2021

1

Earth's geologic **epochs** last 3 million years
Perhaps this fact will bring you to tears
I don't intend to be mean
When I state our Holocene*
Is only about 12,000 years old it appears
(Who wants to see the next one any volunteers)

2

An **epoch** in American history
Was an important event you see
By the end of the civil war
Things were not as before
After the Appomattox* meeting of Grant and Lee

171. TRIAD - 7 DECEMBER 2021

1

A religious **triad** is the holy trinity
All three connected through eternity
Father son or holy ghost
Which do you love the most
They are all the same sacred divinity
(Say a prayer if you've an affinity)

2

A triad of three tones forms a chord
Learn them well to get an award
Chords create the harmony
You'll hear at Carnegie*
With tonal music this will be in accord
(If you get lucky you'll be able to record)

172. BREAK - 8 DECEMBER 2021

1

I had a great deal at stake
It was imperative my habit to **break**
To my wife I'd have to answer
If I developed lung cancer
So I'll quit smoking just for her sake
(Starting at thirteen was a mistake)

2

Chuck Yeager* the sound barrier did **break**
The boom made all the observers quake
Our military it did empower
When we hit 700 miles per hour
We certainly had a great deal at stake
(Thanks goodness he stayed awake)

173. RHINO - 9 DECEMBER 2021

1

The second largest land mammal is the **rhino**
That is even true of the albino
While the elephant is larger
It is not a better charger
I wouldn't want either to step on my toe
(Would I let them? Who me? Why no!)

2

In politics a **RINO*** is not an ungulate
If they were they could not legislate
To elected office they're sworn
They do not possess a horn
Do not trust them at any rate
(This is not up for debate)

174. VIRAL - 10 DECEMBER 2021

1
Covid-19 is an illness that is **viral**
Its emergence created a vicious spiral
Now everyone is grouchy
After taking advice from Fauci
When all we needed was an antiretroviral
(Too bad he was in denial)

2
The video went **viral** on Twitter
When her dog jumped up and bit her
She began to beat the mutt
He bit her again on the butt
Now the dog is X's most popular critter
(I really hope she's not too bitter)

175. CONIC - 11 DECEMBER 2021

At a plane and cone's intersection
It takes a modicum of reflection
To see this form is a **conic**
A parabola that will become iconic
If you can only choose the right section

176. MASSE - 12 DECEMBER 2021

In billiards games they do say
It is hard to execute a **massé***
Like Jackie Gleason* did
The cue ball skidded and slid
Into the side pocket without delay
(Much to Fast Eddie's dismay)

177. SONIC - 13 DECEMBER 2021

1

Beethoven* never heard a boom **sonic**
Which I think is somewhat ironic
For he could not hear
Notes that entered his ear
Whether chromatic or pentatonic
(And yet he remains musically iconic)

2

I was exposed to a **sonic** boom
Too late to exit the room
At 760 miles per hour
The sound had such power
I live with a low-pitched humming tune
(Can't say I'm over the moon)

178. VITAL - 14 DECEMBER 2021

1

Medusa and her three-winged Gorgons*
Could solidify a human being's organs
When they look you in the eye
Your **vital** fluids run dry
Your children will soon be orphans
(Better pray for different fortunes)

2

Cyber spying provides **vital** information
Needed for the protection of our nation
Now Russians and Chinese
Possess greater expertise
Forcing us towards inspired innovation
(Perhaps Israel will provide the inspiration)

179. TRACE - 15 DECEMBER 2021
See 93(2) GAMMA 160(1) CLOCK

1
Deep in outer space
There exists a **trace**
Of subatomic particles
And also antiparticles*
Hope the two never embrace
(Or we'll end up in dire straits)

2
All Mammals need **trace** elements
For healthy myofilaments
Iron Copper Manganese
Ward off nutritional disease
Helping us to avoid impediments
(We've run plenty of experiments)
(Don't worry about the elephants)

180. USING - 16 DECEMBER 2021
See 74 BLEED

After aspirin I started **using**
I noticed that I was bruising
My blood platelets were less sticky*
I developed a huge hickey
So I stopped before I began oozing
(My boyfriend found this amusing)

181. PEACH - 17 DECEMBER 2021

A **Peach** symbolizes a rotund ass
The comparison is a bit low class
A sexual metaphor
Today and long before
The analogy is sexy but crass
(Emoticons these days are a gas)

182. CHAMP - 18 DECEMBER 2021

1

Cassius Clay* became heavyweight **champ**
On boxing he sure left his stamp
As Muhammad Ali
It became clear to see
His image he succeeded to revamp
(The man wasn't stopped by a cramp)

2

I could have been a contender a **champ**
Instead of a useless scamp
Said Brando in On the Waterfront*
He was being particularly blunt
The corrupt union he needed to revamp
(With Eva Marie Saint he planned to decamp)

183. BATON - 19 DECEMBER 2021

1

A beautician came from Saigon
And worked at a fancy salon
When it came to self defense
Her talent was immense
For she was skilled in the use of a **baton**
(No one dare kidnap her komodo dragon)

2

A majorette who twirled her **baton**
Originated from the island of Taiwan
She could make it really spin
Or use it as a rolling pin
To create the most delicious wonton
(The secret ingredient is daikon)

184. BRAKE - 20 DECEMBER 2021

1

While driving I had to suddenly **brake**
To avoid running over a snake
When the reptile did rattle
I took off for Seattle
So fast my car I did forsake
(I hear he still drives it upstate)

2

A friendly Turk by the name of Blake
Was caught in a magnitude 9 earthquake
Lucky to survive unscathed
With all he owned saved
He had to **brake** for his nail's sake
(Next week he plans to hold a wake)

185. PLUCK - 21 DECEMBER 2021

1

In the autumn I shot a duck
Its feathers I did **pluck**
In the cooking it desiccated
Not moist as anticipated
All who ate it quickly up chucked
(Next time I'll won't simmer it in muck)

2

A lad by the name of Simon Tuct
From obscurity was suddenly **pluck**ed
His lifestyle became glossy
Swarmed by paparazzi
So he quit and now he drives a garbage truck
(He secretly likes the smell of the guck)

186. CRAZE - 22 DECEMBER 2021

I assumed it was another passing phase
But I still learned the latest dance **craze**
I tried so hard to twerk
I felt like a jerk
Now I'm in a terpsichorean* haze
(My moves have earned me much praise)

187. GRIPE - 23 DECEMBER 2021

See 136(2) GREAT for 187(2)

1

Clarence just loved to nastily snipe
When a credit card he needed to swipe
He preferred to use cash
Of which he had a stash
Plastic money always made him **gripe**
(He will never understand the hype)

2

The Gipper would never **gripe**
He simply wasn't the type
Short lived George Gipp of football fame
Played multiple positions for Notre Dame
Ronald Reagan that name did swipe*
(Seeing this a tear you may wipe)

188. WEARY - 24 DECEMBER 2021

1

There was an old lady named Mrs Dreary
Of her housework became **weary**
So she abandoned her spouse
Some called her a louse
Now it's said she is feeling more cheery

2
An eccentric old man O'Leary
Developed an interesting theory
He revealed to his daughter
Peel an onion under water
Your eyes will not get teary or **weary**
(Of this suggestion you might be leery)

189. PICKY - 25 DECEMBER 2021

1
There was a horny gal named Vicky
Propositioned by a guy named Mickey
He asked her to make love
She replied heavens above
With whom I screw I am rather **picky**
(Now tell me about your doohickey)

2
When it comes to sex I'm not too **picky**
I am always ready for a quickie
I've no interest in commitment
Only my personal fulfillment
But living this way becomes rather tricky
(And I often end up unpleasantly sticky)

190. ACUTE - 26 DECEMBER 2021

1
Pythagoras* was amazingly astute
He defined when an angle was **acute**
Less than 90 degrees
On this everyone agrees
His pronouncement is well beyond dispute

2
Joe was in **acute** distress
His dismay was hard to suppress
As he gazed in the mirror
It became so much clearer
He looked horrible in his sister's dress
(He needed more work at the bench press)

191. FERRY - 27 DECEMBER 2021

Charon* is the **ferry**man of the dead
Encountering him brings utmost dread
You know you're in a fix
On his **ferry** crossing the Styx
Don't pay with gold but an obol* instead
(Otherwise on his ride you cannot tread)

192. ASIDE - 28 DECEMBER 2021

1
He stepped **aside** to let her pass
So he could get a good look at her ass
He liked what he saw
But she held a hacksaw
And she was far from an innocent lass
(Good thing he didn't harass)

2
Dr Jekyll had a dark side
Which surfaced as Mr Hyde*
He was a marauder
Murder was his fodder
He killed victims after drawing them **aside**

193. TAPIR - 29 DECEMBER 2021

A mammal that's lacking whiskers
Is unable to throw a discus
Lacks the smooth hair of a hare
It's called a **tapir**
And it proudly sports a proboscis

Walking around with a nose trunk
These creatures have a lot of spunk
Here you see a nice **tapir**
They generate water vapor
Into water it's likely to have sunk
(I think this one is rather a hunk)
(I think this limerick is a bunch of bunk)

194. TROLL - 30 DECEMBER 2021
See 219(1) KNOLL for 194(1)

1

Three Billy Goats desired to take a stroll
Across a bridge controlled by a **troll**
Who would not let them pass
Until the big goat butted his ass
Now they feast upon the grassy knoll
(Next time they won't have to pay a toll)

2

Steve loves to **troll** the internet
Posting things his followers won't forget
Employing cyber aggression
To overcome depression
He does this without the slightest regret
(He needs to be called out for his etiquette)

195. UNIFY - 31 DECEMBER 2021

The Central Pacific started in the west
The Union Pacific from the east did press
Rails **unify** in Utah*
Both lines had traveled far
Transportation in America was blessed
(Now the Barons were glad they did invest)

196. REBUS - 1 JANUARY 2022

I came across a quirky cryptogram
On my calculus final exam
I did not have to fuss
To solve the **rebus***
As I used the Razor of Occam*
(The law of parsimony when you're in a jam)

197. BOOST - 2 JANUARY 2022

When I **boost**ed her up on the fence
I didn't think she would take offense
I squeezed her gluteus muscle
Which caused a nasty tussle
Now I'm constantly seeking penitence
(How could I resist something so immense)

198. TRUSS - 3 JANUARY 2022
See 259(1) BRINE for 198(2)

1
A patient by the name of Russ
Consulted a surgeon to discuss
Cancer treatment with hyperthermia*
But the surgeon found a hernia
Now he's wearing an uncomfortable **truss**
(And he's sorry he made such a fuss)

2
Grandma asked me to **truss** the bird
But I thought this idea was absurd
When the stuffing fell out
At me she did shout
You are such an ignorant nerd
(I'll do better with the lemon curd)

199. SIEGE - 4 JANUARY 2022

The 2nd **siege** of Vienna in 1683*
Ended when Ottoman Turks were forced to flee
With the arrival of the detente
Viennese bakers invent the croissant*
Which you'll find today in every bakery
(Try it with a slice of brie or cup of tea)

200. TIGER - 5 JANUARY 2022

1
The Lady or the **Tiger** a short story*
Might end in tragedy or glory
The jealous princess picks a door
The prisoner cannot be sure
If her choice will bring love or an end that's gory
(It serves as one heck of an allegory)

2
Tyger Tyger burning bright
Tyger Tyger in the night
Written by poet William Blake*
When at night he lay awake
Strange that he could not spell **tiger** right

201. BANAL - 6 JANUARY 2022

See 66 PANEL

The Roman sun god's name was Sol
The Phoenician lord of the heavens was Baal
Helios sun god of Peloponnesus
Capable of pyrokinesis*
Modern science makes all these beliefs **banal**
(Say that to a believer you'll start a brawl)

202. SLUMP - 7 JANUARY 2022

1

Her body was much too round and plump
Like Quasimodo* she bore a hump
She had the thickest beard
That needed to be sheared
Quoth she I'm not ugly just in a **slump**
(What does she think I am a chump)

2

The short stop couldn't get pumped
He was in a unremitting **slump**
Time to reverse
This trend adverse
Or next season he is going to get dumped
(To the minors he will be bumped)

203. CRANK - 8 JANUARY 2022

Many thought that he was a **crank**
Some even wondered if he drank
But he circumvented the indignation
With his quantum theory of radiation
And much admiration was earned for Max Plan(c)k*
(A renowned physicist if you've drawn a blank)

204. GORGE - 9 JANUARY 2022

Of seven deadly sins gluttony
Is the one that really plagues me
But if I continue to **gorge** on food
I'll have trouble getting nude
As no one will want to unbutton me
(And yet food still summons me)

205. QUERY - 10 JANUARY 2022

I've always had a desire to **query**
The validity of quantum theory
For if action at a distance*
Is not just concomitance*
The nature of the universe is scary
(Under the covers myself I'll bury)

206. DRINK - 11 JANUARY 2022

1
In Mexico you should never **drink**
Water coming straight from the sink
While it might taste alright
You can't see the parasite
That will cause diarrhea which will stink

2
While at a bar enjoying my **drink**
Over toward me Annabelle did slink
She was tall and blond
But I did not respond
For she was just released from the clink
(And her eye was on my diamond cufflink)

3
I'm in love with my wife Ximena*
For she is a beautiful Latina
She causes me no strife
So I am hers for life
That's why I **drink** her tea of verbena*
(For her I've taken up the ocarina*)

207. FAVOR - 12 JANUARY 2022

1
A tennis pro named Rod Laver*
With fans was always in **favor**
It was at Wimbledon
Four times that he won
That this is true I'm able to aver
(This news all his fans did savor)

2
My ex-wife did me not a **favor**
Swearing in court I tried to enslave her
Although I was actually a nice guy
When she began to shake and cry
All my rights I was forced to waiver

208. ABBEY - 13 JANUARY 2022

At a local Carthusian **Abbey**
The monks are awfully crabby
All take a vow of silence
Which needs strict compliance
So they never can be gabby or blabby

209. TANGY - 14 JANUARY 2022

I make a delicious **tangy** lemon tart
The recipe I strongly refuse to impart
For at almost any venue
You can find it on the menu
But it's only ever served á la carte
(My recipe is really off the chart)
(Yes it will make you pass a **tangy** fart)

210. PANIC - 15 JANUARY 2022

1
While sailing aboard the Titanic
The passengers really did **panic**
When the crew overheard
The ship struck an iceberg
The effect upon all was galvanic
(If only they had on board a mechanic)

2
The word **panic** comes from Greek god Pan*
Who was neither of beast nor of man
But a fertility deity
Not a reality
No one knows how his legend began
(He was only a flash in the pan)

211. SOLAR - 16 JANUARY 2022

1
We traveled to view a **solar** eclipse
It was one of our first and only trips
It should have been romantic
But it turned out to be frantic
When while kissing we bit each others' lips

2
I viewed an interesting documentary
On the many benefits of **solar** energy
But much to my unease
I own too many trees
A lower electric bill I will never see

212. SHIRE - 17 JANUARY 2022

Bilbo Baggins lived in the **shire**
Peace and comfort his main desire
Until Gandalf did bring
A fellowship of the ring*
What an adventure this did inspire
(Of which audiences never do tire)

213. PROXY - 18 JANUARY 2022

I gave my boss my **proxy**
Because he had such moxie
But he voted for termination
Of my directors' application
Isn't that sleazeball foxy

214. POINT - 19 JANUARY 2022

1
A geometric element without dimension
Is a **point**'s definition by convention
If this you can't understand
Your knowledge will not expand
You'll be haunted by deep incomprehension
(Do some research to ease the tension)

2
For you I constantly yearn
Perhaps I'll never learn
My love you do spurn
Why can't you discern
I'm past the **point** of no return
(The lament of a slow swimming sperm)

215. ROBOT - 20 JANUARY 2022

1
The human race is much better off
For Laws of **Robot**ics by Azimov*
If you live all alone
With a **robot** of your own
At these three laws you should never scoff

2
Robby the **Robot** served our crew tea
In the movie Forbidden Planet* you see
Beautiful Morbius' daughter
Knew all the **robot** taught her
And she was gorgeous everyone did agree

216. PRICK - 21 JANUARY 2022
See 51 LINEN

Her finger on the spinning wheel she did **prick**
It could have been a disastrous fatal stick
For the wicked Maleficent
Cursed Aurora the innocent
But she survived due to a hibernation schtick*

The situation was truly alarming
Before the arrival of Prince Charming
Her red lips he kissed quick
While handing her his throbbing **prick**
Now she's happy making love and never darning

217. WINCE - 22 JANUARY 2022

1

There once was a very handsome prince
Of marriage the queen tried to convince
He was offered a choice
Elaine Cindy or Joyce
But all of them just made him **wince**
(None of them knew to use mouth rinse)

2

My date cooked for me lamb and quince
Upon tasting it I had to **wince**
For this bad fare
I really don't care
I would much rather have a blintz*

218. CRIMP - 23 JANUARY 2022

1

A hair stylist my hair did **crimp**
But she was busy and did skimp
Her efforts did fail
For if I had a tail
I know that I'd look like a chimp
(At least I know how to primp)

2

Please do not **crimp** my style
With the gal I am trying to defile
If you dare interfere
It will become clear
That my intentions are rather vile
(That's going to make her incredibly hostile)

219. KNOLL - 24 JANUARY 2022

See 194(1) TROLL for 219(2)

1

I met my lovely wife Nicole
While sitting on a grassy **knoll**
When she sat near me
I could quickly foresee
To know her would be my life's goal
(I meant it with my heart and soul)

2

Conspiracy theories I do not extoll
That shots fired from the grassy **knoll***
Killed John Kennedy
Monumentally
Lee Harvey Oswald dealt the fatal blow

220. SUGAR - 25 JANUARY 2022

Another name for **sugar** is glucose
There's also fructose sucrose and lactose
Which of these four sweeties
Is the worst for diabetes
Probably the one that you love the most
(With pies it's hard not to be engrossed)

221. WHACK - 26 JANUARY 2022

1

On her part it was a foolish act
Completely lacking in any tact
When near her I bent over
I was smacked by a bulldozer
For she had given me a tremendous **whack**
(I deserved it for making a wisecrack)

2
The math problem proved difficult to solve
Its solution took decades to evolve
But when Pascal* took a **whack** at it
All were glad he had a crack at it
Thereafter this problem came to a resolve

222. MOUNT - 27 JANUARY 2022

1
In 79 AD **Mount** Vesuvius did erupt
The death of 16,000 was abrupt
Many died of asphyxiation
Others by cremation
Pompeii* it did completely disrupt
(If only they hadn't been so corrupt)

2
Edmund Hillary first to summit **Mount** Everest*
To accomplish this he had to be the cleverest
Oh and by the way
It was with his sherpa Norgay
Later the summit many have traversed

3
The circumstances I will try to recount
When on top of her I did **mount**
She was completely receptive
Because I wore a contraceptive
So we screwed too many times to count
(Just don't ask for her account)
(In truth I am a veritable fount)

223. PERKY - 28 JANUARY 2022

Many thought he was a turkey
Because his movements were jerky
But he was not spastic
Just enthusiastic
In reality he was merely **perky**

224. COULD - 29 JANUARY 2022

1
I would or I should or I **could**
All verbs that are misunderstood
But the study of grammar
Is lacking in glamor
And would do me absolutely no good
(There are worse things I have withstood)

2
There was a cantankerous recluse
So masochistic he would self-abuse
Flagellation his game
Why he **could**n't refrain
For he really was incredibly obtuse
(Don't ask him about this noose)

225. WRUNG - 30 JANUARY 2022

When we were very young
Her dainty neck I **wrung**
Now we're fully grown
I've tried to atone
But with me she's always high strung

226. LIGHT - 31 JANUARY 2022

1
Its rate is out of sight
So quick is the speed of **light**
But please don't dote on
The speed of a photon*
186,000 miles per second that's right

2
I will only drink Coors **Light**
Any other beer does not taste right
But offer me liquor
I'll accept even quicker
For that to me would be a delight
(But I've no interest in a beer flight)

227. THOSE - 1 FEBRUARY 2022

The plural of that is **those**
Useful to know writing prose
But to write a limerick
That wouldn't do the trick
For they are much harder to compose
(Creating them has sent me into throes)

228. MOIST - 2 FEBRUARY 2022

Our eyes were **moist** with joy of success
For finally we had made progress
Our son graduated college
With a modicum of knowledge
And finally moved out to his own address
(Why this is wondrous I need not stress)

229. SHARD - 3 FEBRUARY 2022

Star Trek hero Captain Picard
Was held in highest regard
An explosion did surprise
On the USS Enterprise
And he was hit in the ass with a **shard**
(No matter what he always went the extra yard)

230. PLEAT - 4 FEBRUARY 2022

When wearing your **pleat**ed miniskirt
You should never ever flirt
The skirt is too short
For the panties you sport
And will place all the boys on high alert
(Even the gay ones may convert)

231. ALOFT - 5 FEBRUARY 2022

Whenever uncle Joe coughed
The sound seemed fairly soft
But when his mouth he covered
His bald spot we discovered
For his hairpiece would fly **aloft**

232. SKILL - 6 FEBRUARY 2022

It does not require great **skill**
For the blue whale to eat so much krill*
The crustacean is so small
Whales don't see them at all
Mouth open wide their hunger they fulfill
(I wonder if they ever put them on the grill)

233. ELDER - 7 FEBRUARY 2022

The very first time I beheld her
It was clear she was my **elder**
For Methuselah's wife*
Also had a long life
To outlive him is what compelled her

234. FRAME - 8 FEBRUARY 2022

1
Does the universe have a **frame**
Boundaries that one can proclaim
Or is it boundless
This does confound us
We'll never know and that is a shame
(Though really that does not change our aim)

2
At first I thought she was playing a game
She was to me an old flame
When she murdered her brother
She blamed another
It was me she was trying to **frame**
(Vengeance for my attempt to defame)

235. HUMOR - 9 FEBRUARY 2022

1
We kids waited for the Good **Humor** man*
For his ice cream we all were a big fan
His bells made us sigh
When his truck came by
Toward the man dressed in white we all ran
(This is where my obsession with ice cream began)

2
On my chest x-ray was found a tumor
Causing me to lose my sense of **humor**
When it was deemed benign
I popped open a fine wine
Thankful it was just a pseudotumor*
(A malignancy was merely a rumor)

236. PAUSE - 10 FEBRUARY 2022
See 164 BRING

As he refuses to walk through doors
There's much concern about Santa Claus
Sliding down the chimney
When he is anything but skinny
Should be reason enough to give him **pause**
(Besides that he is breaking many laws)

237. ULCER - 11 FEBRUARY 2022

1
A peptic **ulcer** tells quite a story
Caused by Helicobacter Pylori*
A rather tiny bacteria
Living in the cafeteria
For these bugs our stomach is their quarry
(What did you eat quick take inventory)

2
I developed an **ulcer** on my cock
For me this was a big shock
No doubt it was Phyllis
Who gave to me syphilis
Apparently she caught it from Jacques
(Oh please help me what do I do doc)

238. ULTRA - 12 FEBRUARY 2022

It is true Rabid **ultra-**nationalism
Said to be one form of radicalism
A major cause of World War One
A reason the war had begun
At a time we could trust journalism

239. ROBIN - 13 FEBRUARY 2022

See 248 THORN 260 CLOTH

The American **robin** is a songbird
Cheer up cheer up its song is heard
One once plucked a thorn
From the crown Jesus did adorn*
That's why its breast is red it is averred
(A group of them is a round not a herd)

240. CYNIC - 14 FEBRUARY 2022

In ancient Athens all **cynics** did agree
To make **Cynic**ism a philosophy*
Diogenes went too far
Living in a ceramic jar
From all possessions he remained completely free
(Certainly not a lifestyle for you or me)

241. AROMA - 15 FEBRUARY 2022

1
In the Big Apple I visited the MOMA*
On entering I detected a great **aroma**
Emanating from the restaurant
Why they were serving elephant
The recipe was provided by the Shona*

2
The lovely **aroma** was familiar to me
But what it was no one could agree
My olfaction was not swayed
Until the aroma did pervade
Why it's vanilla it was plain to see
(Actually my olfactory apparatus cannot see)

242. CAULK - 16 FEBRUARY 2022

In my house there are no windows to **caulk**
Nor is there a door you need to lock
It is made of ice and snow
Where it is ten degrees below
That's why my igloo is not made of rock
(I would still prefer it if you knock)
(Though you'll never catch me in a frock)

243. SHAKE - 17 FEBRUARY 2022

1
As a teen rock and roll was in my soul
At that time the only music I'd extol
Bill Haley and the Comets
Recorded with such promise
Notably their classic **Shake** Rattle and Roll*
(It was especially good when I smoked a bowl)

2
All of a sudden I began to **shake**
I thought I was in an earthquake
My body did freeze
Its my Parkinson's Disease*
Soup today was clearly a mistake

244. DODGE - 18 FEBRUARY 2022

1

Madam Theresa Lafarge*
A woman you want to **dodge**
For she is the philistine
Sitting near the guillotine
Waiting for your head to dislodge
(Knitting you a sweater that's entirely too large)

2

Romeo had not as of yet
Met her cousin Tybalt Capulet
Whom at Romeo will charge
With a sword Romeo will **dodge**
For killing Tybalt he will lose Juliet
(And both families will bear much regret)

245. SWILL - 19 FEBRUARY 2022

1

He **swill**ed the broth around in a pot
But the Campbell soup never got hot
No it never got warm
The stovetop refused to perform
To turn on the gas the old codger forgot

2

If you have some time to kill
Come visit me at my still
I make moonshine
I can't offer fine wine
But you can have all the booze you can **swill**
(I hope you have drafted your will)

246. TACIT - 20 FEBRUARY 2022

There was a young man from Ghent
Who thought he had her **tacit** consent
Either she was not clear
Or he did not hear
Neither understood the others intent
(Needless to say there was strong discontent)

247. OTHER - 21 FEBRUARY 2022

See 307 PLANT 359(1+2) DONOR 390(1) LIVER for 247(1)

1

I'm not trying to make you laugh
But you are just like my **other** half
How can I begin
You are like my twin
Perhaps you are my holograph*
(Or you are my homograft*)

2

I traveled from one place to an**other**
Trying to locate my mother
But she moved away
Some say to Bombay
And is living with my twin brother
(Her identity will I ever discover)

248. THORN - 22 FEBRUARY 2022

See 239 ROBIN 260 CLOTH for 248(1)

1

It was clearly a symbol of scorn
That Jesus was forced to have worn
The king of the Jews
Of blasphemy accused
Forced to wear a crown made of **thorn**
(Poor Mary was left forlorn)

2
It is a real **thorn** in my side
From which I'm unable to hide
It grabbed my genitals
With its tentacles
I pray it goes out with the tide

249. TROVE - 23 FEBRUARY 2022

I found their treasure **trove**
Buried deep in the wild grove
By a pack of thieves
I put it up my sleeves
And hid it all in a cove
(Now I'll forever have to rove)
(Lest I'm discovered by Jove*)

250. BLOKE - 24 FEBRUARY 2022

Before he had his stroke
He was an extraordinary **bloke**
Now he's lost in a haze
Staring with fixed gaze
Just like us ordinary folk

251. VIVID - 25 FEBRUARY 2022

See 298(2) CHUNK 387(1) MADAM for 251(1)

1
She was having a very **vivid** dream
A garden in full bloom it did seem
The Garden of Eden
Before the apple was eaten
And she was with celestial cherubim
(All of it had an otherworldly gleam)
(This idea has now run out of steam)

2
She had such a **vivid** imagination
But completely lacked discrimination
An obsessive compulsive
A flagrant impulsive
But she was fine when on her medication
(Otherwise she was in need of sedation)

252. SPILL - 26 FEBRUARY 2022

1
The crowds **spill**ed into the street
Ignoring the tropical heat
Cheering for Fidel
Soon their lives will be hell
Democracy in Cuba is now obsolete

2
A man by the name of Wilk
Spilled a bottle of milk
His cat could care less
About all the mess
To kitty it tasted smooth as silk

253. CHANT - 27 FEBRUARY 2022

See 384(2) VOICE

To Roman Catholics the Gregorian **chant***
In the present has remained extant
It is always monophonic
Which makes it quite ironic
To sing in harmony the church choir can't
(To God they are a sycophant)

254. CHOKE - 28 FEBRUARY 2022

1
At first I thought it was a joke
When suddenly Debbie did **choke**
In Debbie Does Dallas*
She chokes on a phallus
After which she was unable to smoke
(So she gave the poor guy a poke)

2
That day I never spoke up
For fear that I would **choke** up
Marry me to my fiancé
I was unable to say
So she cried and then we broke up
(All these tears I'd like to soak up)
(I think it's time for me to toke up)
(Perhaps it's time I woke up)

255. RUPEE - 1 MARCH 2022

The currency known as the **rupee**
Used by Indians and Pakistani
81 rupees to the dollar
Why so many live in squalor
And there are so few bourgeoisie

256. NASTY - 2 MARCH 2022

1
A soprano who lives in Tallahassee
Has a voice both **nasty** and raspy
For she sings through her nose
Which alters her air flows
She'll sing at the MET* after rhinoplasty

2
It was a terribly **nasty** deed
The Nazis ultimately agreed
Sterilize the mentally ill*
Their quotas to fulfill
So they would be unable to breed

257. MOURN - 3 MARCH 2022

See 83 LAPEL for 257(2)

1
Mozart's death the world did **mourn**
Leaving all his admirers forlorn
He composed his own requiem*
Most beautiful of the millennium
This music his funeral did adorn
(Have you tried playing it on the french horn)

2
When a Jew dies it is time to **mourn**
To express grief one's lapel is torn
Sitting Shiva* for seven days
Everyone grieves and prays
To this manner of bereavement they are sworn

258. AHEAD - 4 MARCH 2022

1
In the alphabet A comes **ahead** of Z
If learned well one can get a degree
An MD or a PhD
In medicine or philosophy
Learning it early seems to be the key

2
One never knows what lies **ahead**
Will you be alive or dead
Live each day as your last they say
This is not a cliche
Your inhibitions you will need to shed
(Be not afraid of the path you will tread)

259. BRINE - 5 MARCH 2022
See 198 TRUSS for 259(1)

1
Before cooking your bird it's best to **brine**
In a strong solution of salt coarse or fine
And if you stuff that bird
It would be best to gird
With a lightweight cord of twine
(With it perhaps a glass of wine)

2
The oldest shipwreck of all time
For 2400 years was sunk in the **brine**
The ancient Greek ship Odysseus*
Since 400 BC was oblivious
In Davy Jones Locker* covered in slime

260. CLOTH - 6 MARCH 2022
See 239 ROBIN 248(1) THORN

The Shroud of Turin* has been adored
As the burial **cloth** of Christ our lord
Bearing the negative image of a man
This holy relic studied with a scan
And in many other ways explored

261. HOARD - 7 MARCH 2022

A recognized delusional disorder
That of the animal **hoard**er
Mimicking a squirrel's behavior
Copying Noah the animal savior
Their home is pervaded with much ordure*
(Keeping the house clean requires ardor)

262. SWEET - 8 MARCH 2022

1

There was a nice lady named Ruth
Who had a persistent **sweet** tooth
When her blood sugar did double
She knew it was trouble
So she stopped consuming vermouth
(Oh the pain of losing your youth)

2

A song named **Sweet** Caroline
Was released in 1969
Victory anthem of the Red Sox*
A song that really truly rocks
For Neil Diamond it was a gold mine
(And one of his best-selling songs of all time)

263. MONTH - 9 MARCH 2022

1

A **month** is a measure of time
Which is not easy to define
Thirty days approximately
Discounting February
Remember how many days in each with a rhyme*

2
My rent is due at the end of each **month**
So I'm afraid I will need to be blunt
I lack sufficient cash
My apartment is filled with trash
What should I say when my landlord does confront
(I'll have to disappear for my next stunt)

3
I don't mention this to confront
Nor are my words intended to affront
But with reference to the moon
I'm completely in tune
For it orbits the earth just once a **month**

264. LAPSE - 10 MARCH 2022

1
At a formal dinner her manners did **lapse**
When they served creamed mushroom caps
And when dinner was over
I don't know what drove her
To eat everyone's leftover scraps
(Perhaps she had imbibed too much Schnapps)

2
There was a very handsome prince
Who suffered a **lapse** of conscience
For he had an affair
With a married maiden fair
But has had nothing to do with her since

265. WATCH - 11 MARCH 2022

1

Paul Revere was on the **watch**
For a lantern hung in a belfry arch
One if by land and two if by sea*
How the British arrive will be the key
For the Continental Army to march

2

I was frequently warned to **watch** out
Cheating at poker this was about
Never again in their good graces
After I pulled 5 aces
Now my honesty is always in doubt
(Save for my wife who is most devout)

266. TODAY - 12 MARCH 2022

1

Today is the first day of the rest of my life
I felt this was true since I met my wife
With children we are blessed
Achieving our final quest
I celebrate the joy with which we are rife
(Hold on honey where did you get that knife)

2

Today is the only time of which to be sure
For it's never certain we'll be granted more
So make the most of it
To your loved ones admit
How your love for them will always be secure

267. FOCUS - 13 MARCH 2022

1

I asked my internist to **focus**
On finding the right diagnosis
Without one it seems to me
There would be no guarantee
The treatment offered won't be hocus pocus

2

Newborn babies for months cannot **focus**
Later we lose vision from atherosclerosis*
And I also dare to report
When our arms get too short*
We need glasses to see the star Canopus

268. SMELT - 14 MARCH 2022

1

To make steel you need to **smelt** iron ore
You remove oxygen in fire that does roar
At 3000 degrees Fahrenheit
Above iron's melting point that's right
The result is not liquid but a solid core
(I learned from Hephaestus* on his tour)

2

The tiny California Delta **smelt**
In San Francisco estuary has dwelt
Larger fish on them rely
Now endangered in short supply
Will this problem resolve when the icebergs melt
(What a lousy hand they've been dealt)

269. TEASE - 15 MARCH 2022

1
Tweety bird loved to **tease** and pester
The persnickety feline Sylvester
Despite the puddy cat's pride
He's always the losing side
No he never had the chance to digest her

2
She is known to be a cock **tease**
About that every man agrees
All the guys have tried
But unless some have lied
Her desires none were able to appease

270. CATER - 16 MARCH 2022

We strive to **cater** to everyone's taste
Food prepared with panache and grace
Be so kind as to ask your waiter
For monkey brain or alligator
Ordering hamburger is considered a disgrace
(Ask for ketchup and they'll bring out the mace)

271. MOVIE - 17 MARCH 2022

See 54(2) BOOBY for 271(1)

1
I asked a gal to join me for a **movie**
She said that that would be groovy
But the usher threw me out
When she began to shout
Obscenities when I squeezed her booby
(Guess it's time to light up a doobie*)

2
With streaming **movie**s over the internet
Movie theaters we can now all forget
Except for the popcorn
And select offerings of porn
Where we watch **movie**s has been reset
(And don't get me started on video cassette)

272. SAUTE - 18 MARCH 2022

See 284 STOVE

When cooking I really have to say
The best meals are ones you **sauté**
Leave it to the French
This method to entrench
Its universal use in cooking today

273. ALLOW - 19 MARCH 2022

1
Ladies and gents **allow** me to introduce
The most powerful Greek god Zeus
In Greek mythology
He reigns as chief deity
So I suggest your praise be profuse
(Lest he turn you into a spruce)

2
As a child I was never **allow**ed
To get mixed up in a crowd
Before the Salk vaccine*
Not available till I was a teen
By polio we were all cowed

274. RENEW - 20 MARCH 2022

You must sleep for your body to **renew**
So you can start the next day anew
During non-REM* sleep
Our memories we get to keep
REM sleep dreaming alters what we construe
(Don't ask how you ended up in Peru)

275. THEIR - 21 MARCH 2022

See those artists over there
For **their** work I do not care
His work is too spare
Hers is hard to bare
To tell them this I'd never dare
(I guess that's neither here nor there)

276. SLOSH - 22 MARCH 2022

First I noticed the swash
Then I heard the **slosh**
Ocean water filling my boat
I wondered could it still float
By then I was almost awash
(GOSH!)

277. PURGE - 23 MARCH 2022
See 93(1) GAMMA for 277(1)

1
That day I really did splurge
When my monkey did urge
I eat bananas with him
I filled up to the brim
Now I need a laxative to **purge**
(Please don't look at what will emerge)

2
Today I went to confession
To **purge** myself of aggression
But the priest simply said
See a psychiatrist instead
You just have a weird obsession

278. CHEST - 24 MARCH 2022

I was terribly stressed
By a sharp pain in my **chest**
The doctor said I'd die
Of an acute MI*
Then he asked me to get undressed

Then and there I became distressed
By the opinion he had expressed
When I took off my shirt
The diagnosis was overt
There was a nipple ring in my breast
(I hope he was a little impressed)
(The problem was never in my **chest**)

279. DEPOT - 25 MARCH 2022

See 399 MIDGE for 279(2)

1

I bet you didn't know
We all have fat **depot**s
For men it's abdominal
For women gluteal femoral
That's where that darn stuff will grow
(From our pants we overflow)

2

There once was Latino
Who visited an army **depot**
Where he caught dengue fever*
After becoming a receiver
Of the bite of an Aedes mosquito
(He bit it back quid pro quo)

280. EPOXY - 26 MARCH 2022

Epoxy resin use is extensive
These materials are not expensive
Used in fiberglass and polyester
Invented by a college professor
Its applications are comprehensive
(About using it I'm apprehensive)

281. NYMPH - 27 MARCH 2022

1

A **nymph** is never a runty male
She's always a human size female
The Nereids* number fifty
Poseidon they accompany
Sirens* are half birds with a tail
(You may see them all if you set sail)

2
In the mythological spirit world
Nymphs flew around and twirled
In our tangible world you and I
Can observe a dragonfly
The only nymphs that now around us whirl
(From our plane the rest were hurled*)

282. FOUND - 28 MARCH 2022

1
One day while walking I **found**
A diamond ring on the ground
Searching for its owner
It turned out I had known her
It was my ex-wife and that did astound*

2
As a kid one day I **found***
A small brown ball firm and round
I thought it was a berry
But was told by my friend Jerry
It was a goat turd that I had almost downed

283. SHALL - 29 MARCH 2022

The ten commandments does not uses **shall**
It's unclear what was the rational
To use only shalt nots
Instead of **shall** nots
Perhaps that was better for morale
(Biblical grammarians were more formal)

284. STOVE - 30 MARCH 2022
See 272 SAUTE

For years I conscientiously strove
To learn how to cook on a **stove**
Yet everything I'd sauté
Tasted just like clay
For I forgot to use a garlic clove
(Knowing now what a treasure trove)

285. LOWLY - 31 MARCH 2022
See 128 FLING 164(2) BRING

Sir Lancelot bowed **lowly** before his king
To be knighted what a wonderful thing
But King Arthur was unaware
That his wife sweet Gwenivere
With Lancelot was having a fling
(When he learned oh what a sting)

286. SNOUT - 1 APRIL 202

1

Dashing French officer Cyrano de Bergerac*
Expert swordsman never first to attack
Famous for his long **snout**
His poetry he loves to tout
But with Cousin Roxanne he's on the wrong track

2

There is a young wooden boy you may know
Who goes by the name of Pinocchio
His **snout** grows when he tells a lie
The elongation makes him cry
Soon a real boy conversion he'll undergo
(He'll know what it's like to stub his toe)

The Great Schnozzola Jimmy Durante
His large **snout** was evident to see
An actor singer comedian
A talented popular man
Was his sense of smell better than you and me
(Perhaps Mrs Calabash* holds the key)

287. TROPE - 2 APRIL 2022

A **trope*** is just a figure of speech
A type of cliche I would never teach
Using **tropes** isn't wrong
When writing a song
But avoid them I humbly beseech
(It's even worse when you screech)

288. FEWER - 3 APRIL 2022

I've always wondered if it was by design
That we have a concise less than sign*
Why not a sign for **fewer** than
Is there a symbolic ban
Or did the **fewer** than sign just not align
(But the greater than sign is simply divine)

289. SHAWL - 4 APRIL 2022

See 141(2) DUCHY 169(2) USHER

She was at least six feet tall
The most seductive of them all
When I picked her up at eight
For a family dinner date
She was wearing a pashmina* **shawl**
(And nothing else at all)

290. NATAL - 5 APRIL 2022

See 0 CIGAR 122 COMET

Most people have a **natal** star
Mark Twain's birth was bizarre*
Halley's comet visited his cradle
That same comet proved to be fatal
So give Samuel Clemens a cigar
(In heaven he has that and caviar)

291. COMMA - 6 APRIL 2022

If you are writing to your momma
Use good grammar use a **comma**
For your letters could betray
And cause her much dismay
Your smoking too much marijuana
(To join in she might wanna)

292. FORAY - 7 APRIL 2022

The Vikings of Norway
Into Scotland did **foray**
But when not fighting
They were often flyting*
The rap battles of their day
(Cover your ears I pray)

293. SCARE - 8 APRIL 2022

1
With only you I'd like to share
What gives me a horrible **scare**
The creature from the black lagoon
Werewolves howling at the moon
To horror movies don't take me I declare
(I can't even handle your fierce glare)

2
A creepy guy named Pierre
At women would always stare
They felt the need to beware
But they wouldn't **scare**
If he only would comb his hair

294. STAIR - 9 APRIL 2022

1
There once was a man named Pierre
Who was a multi-millionaire
Now his heirs weep
For he was too cheap
To repair what was a broken **stair**
(He even had on hand a step to spare)

2
There once was a man named McNair*
Who was screwing a gal on the **stair**
When the banister broke
He doubled the stroke
And finished her off in mid-air

295. BLACK - 10 APRIL 2022

1
In western movies there is always a fight
And it is usually quite a sight
The bad guy in a **black** hat
Portrayed as a dirty rat
Always loses to the hat that is white

2
Black panthers are actually jaguars
Not the ones that are British cars
They have retractable claws
Their sense of smell deserves applause
They are predatory superstars

3
Angela Davis a **black** feminist
Also a highly radical activist
A **Black** Panther communist
On the FBI's most wanted list
Has a Mayflower ancestor what a twist*

4
I have a granddaughter strange*
In her skills there is wide range
Her last name is **Black**
She likes to talk back
I hope she doesn't ever change
(This limerick I'm sure she'll rearrange)

296. SQUAD - 11 APRIL 2022

1
Four congresswoman who are very odd
Are referred to as the **squad**
Their stupidity
Will go down in history
Each one is a socialist clod

2
An agent of the Mossad*
An elite counterterrorism **squad**
Is intensively trained
Hardly ever restrained
In acting for Israel and its God

297. ROYAL - 12 APRIL 2022

Prince Harry was a British **royal**
Until Megan Markle his title did spoil
They abandoned the **royal** family
Due to Megan's vanity
Thereby proving themselves disloyal

The current British Prince **royal**
William for his title did not toil
Not earned through merit
One he did inherit
And one he must never despoil

298. CHUNK - 13 APRIL 2022

See 251(1) VIVID 387(1) MADAM for 298(2)

1

Tony loved to go out and spelunk*
Exploring limestone caves that had sunk
Impressed with stalactites
And also with stalagmites
From each he cut off a large **chunk**
(Especially fun when he was drunk)

2

From a single **chunk** of clay
God made Adam one bright day
Then took from his rib
Material to make a glib
Female from his DNA
(Thereby introducing foreplay)

299. MINCE - 14 APRIL 2022

1

I never would **mince** words
To me that would be absurd
This leads to arguments
Of this I am convinced
But it's important that I be heard
(Good communication is preferred)

2

At his coronation Henry V did eat
Mince meat pies that were a treat
With a crisp pastry crust
Sweet flavor and robust
But they were really a problem to excrete
(The crusts contained too much wheat)

300. SHAME - 15 APRIL 2022

1

It is a **shame** youth is wasted on the young
An expression often lamented and sung
Elderly recite this catchy phrase
While looking back on better days
This is the group I am now among
(Old age upon me has sprung)

2

This song recorded by a man whose name
Was Fats Domino* received great acclaim
A recriminatory yet catchy song
Which topped the pop charts so long
Ain't That a **Shame** made tears fall like rain
(You're the one to blame)

301. CHEEK - 16 APRIL 2022

1

In college we would sometimes streak
Thereby exposing each buttock **cheek**
Now older we'd never dare
To show our derriere
For we are no longer proud of our physique
(About this we no longer wish to speak)

2

When you and I go dancing **cheek** to **cheek**
Like Fred and Ginger across the floor we sweep
We are acutely aware
To them we can't compare
For when we dance you can hear our bones creak
(But we've still got a great technique)
(You're in no place to critique)

302. AMPLE - 17 APRIL 2022

1
George received an injury hippocampal*
At a soccer match where he was tr**ample**d
This caused amnesia
And chronic paresthesia*
But what was left of his cerebrum was **ample**

2
His wife's figure was rotund and **ample**
Her wares she wished for me to s**ample**
But I like my women slim
What a fix that put me in
I'm so proud I could set a moral ex**ample**

303. FLAIR - 18 APRIL 2022

A restaurant on Trafalgar square
Had a quintessential European **flair**
Although the food was great
Whatever it was that I ate
Threw my bowels into disrepair

304. FOYER - 19 APRIL 2022

I always get into trouble with my spouse
Wearing muddy boots entering the house
Because that annoys her
She hollers leave them in the **foyer**
When admonishing me she really screams and shouts
(She often tells me I'm such a louse)

305. CARGO - 20 APRIL 2022

The ship was carrying a **cargo** of crude oil
A Russian tanker attempting sanctions to foil
Its movements were clandestine
Our allies no longer invest in
Russian crude oil sales that they wish to spoil

306. OXIDE - 21 APRIL 2022

Most of the earth's crust consists of **oxide**s
One can prove this by studying rockslides
Below earth's crust furthermore
Is the mantle and the core
The core too hot to make any dioxides

307. PLANT - 22 APRIL 2022

See 247(1) OTHER 359(1+2) DONOR 390(1) LIVER

There once was a fellow named Grant
Who in his garden did foolishly **plant**
A Venus fly trap
Now he's unable to snap
His fingers until he gets a trans**plant**

308. OLIVE - 23 APRIL 2022

1
Composer Giacomo Puccini*
Never put an **olive** in his martini
After writing Madam Butterfly
He needed to get high
So he drank four with his linguini
(But he was no match for Rossini)

2
Speaking of very delicious **olive** oil
Olives grow well in Mediterranean soil
But California oil is best
Because it is cold pressed
Extra Virgin requires so much toil
(All the work makes me recoil)

3
Olive Oyl was Popeye's sweet girl
He loved the way her hair would curl
When for her he got an itch
He would eat his spinach
So over his head Bluto he could hurl

309. INERT - 24 APRIL 2022

1
In my backyard I found a dead opossum*
I had no idea where it could have come from
It lay there **inert**
No effort did it exert
I left - returned - it was gone - boy am I dumb

2
Never inhale a noble gas
That will put you on your ass
Asphyxiation is insidious
Your death would be hideous
For all 6 gasses are **inert** alas *

There are 6 known noble or **inert** gasses
That I learned about in chemistry classes
If you should swallow any
I'll bet you a pretty penny
You'll never know when it passes out of your asses

310. ASKEW - 25 APRIL 2022

A picture hanger from Timbuktu
Always hangs paintings **askew**
So if it's him you hire
You must insist and require
He measure carefully so they hang true
(And then be sure to leave a good review)

311. HEIST - 26 APRIL 2022

Willie Sutton* was chronically enticed
To enter banks so money he could **heist**
Why rob banks they did quiz
He said that's where the money is
But no amount of money ever sufficed
(Everything these days is so highly priced)

312. SHOWN - 27 APRIL 2022

After she had **shown** me to the door
I realized she was not a whore
So I rechecked the address
My mistake I did confess
It seems I was on the wrong floor
(Her discretion I did earnestly implore)

313. ZESTY - 28 APRIL 2022

I was at a complete loss
Her meatloaf I wanted to toss
But she didn't understand
Her cooking was too bland
And in need of a real **zesty** sauce*
(Truly it tasted like moss)

314. TRASH - 29 APRIL 2022

1
My teeth I did forcefully gnash
It was him I wanted to smash
My roommate is a putz
Perhaps he's even nuts
Most likely he's contemptuous low life **trash**
(It's our taste in music over which we clash)

2
It certainly was a mishmash
Over which my wife and I did clash
For my rubber duckie collection
I had such deep affection
But to her it was nothing but **trash**
(Now I'll have to keep a hidden stash)

315. LARVA - 30 APRIL 2022
See 99 MOULT

Insect larva comes from an egg
Wingless worms without a leg
A chrysalis after it molts
From its cocoon it revolts
You might find them in the dregs of any keg

316. FORGO - 1 MAY 2022

1
Ascetics are intensely austere
Their abstinences are not a veneer
You don't want to know
All the things they **forgo**
But celibacy is of the most severe

2
I arrived on the mountain plateau
At the last moment I chose to **forgo**
For I became stiff
Almost jumping off the cliff
Hang gliding is not for me you know
(Notably when my guide screamed look out below)

317. STORY - 2 MAY 2022

See 169(1) USHER 380(1)SEVER

Papa please tell me a **story**
One that's not scary or gory
I'm certain you know
One from Edgar Allan Poe
One that he wrote just for me

The bedtime **story** to tell that I chose
Is called the Emperor's New Clothes*
Anderson's funny parable
Was the emperor invisible
NO! His privates were fully exposed
(This story is not Edgar Allan Poe's)

318. HAIRY - 3 MAY 2022

1
The Abominable Snowman is **hairy**
Which is what makes him so scary
In Asia he's called Yeti
It's uncertain if yet he
Will ever be able to marry
(Many a suitor is often wary)

2
Once when I was very young
I developed a **hairy** tongue*
I was taken aback
When it turned black
Something furry to my tongue had clung
(I shouldn't have eaten that cow dung)

319. TRAIN - 4 MAY 2022

1
It's my mind I need to **train**
To get confidence into my brain
To become an entertainer
As a brave lion trainer
I would have to really be insane
(But gosh life is just so inane)

2
When I was two my mom did explain
It was time for me to potty **train**
At four I still wear a diaper
For I am just very hyper
Too impatient for my poop to retain

320. HOMER - 5 MAY 2022

See 359(2) DONOR

All the baseball fans of Mudville*
Were looking for a big thrill
To watch Casey hit a **homer**
Instead they got a groaner
His third strike their joy did kill

321. BADGE - 6 MAY 2022

1
American author Stephan Crane*
Wrote a novel that was humane
The Red **Badge** of Courage
All war he did discourage
By disclosing private Henry Fleming's shame

2
There was a girl scout named Madge
Who wanted to earn a merit **badge**
But there was none for cosmetics
And she hated athletics
So she quit and went on a hajj*
(I think school she was trying to dodge)

322. MIDST - 7 MAY 2022

In the **midst** of this terrible war
Vladimir Putin all Ukrainians abhor
For he invaded with full force
Showing absolutely no remorse
Killing Ukrainian civilians by the score
(Since then he has killed many more)

323. CANNY - 8 MAY 2022

There once was a fellow named Manny
Who proved to be rather **canny**
At a famous art museum
He hid behind a mausoleum
And ran off with a Modigliani*
(Nowadays he goes about wearing Armani)

324. SHINE - 9 MAY 2022

1

I will love you come rain or come **shine**
And I really want you to be mine
Agree to be my wife
I will love you all my life
But if you don't your name I will malign
(That I am crazy about you this is not a sign)

2

Light on earth is from sweet sun**shine**
Solar photons are emitted all the time
From its chromosphere
Reaching our atmosphere
The light and warmth provided are sublime

325. GECKO - 10 MAY 2022

1

A Bolivian god an Ekeko*
While hiking spotted a **gecko**
He followed it down a trail
And grabbed it by the tail
Now he is painting like El Greco*

2

Although it has not brought it fame
Only one animal can say its own name
I bet you didn't know
It is the gecko
That only a lizard can is such a shame
(Perhaps it's only an imitation game)
(Can parrots and crows do the same)

326. FARCE - 11 MAY 2022
See 148 PITHY

Shakespeare's Taming of the Shrew is a **farce**
Its plot is fun but challenging to parse
Petruchio tricks Katrina to marry
Then makes her less contrary
Now she is no longer spouting shrewish remarks
(Between her and her husband still fly sparks)

327. SLUNG - 12 MAY 2022

The fate of King Saul's nation once hung
Upon shepherd's son David who was young
Philistines demand single combat
Against a giant scary to look at
David killed Goliath with a stone he had **slung**
(If you're very literal you might prefer flung)

328. TIPSY - 13 MAY 2022

1
There once was a fellow from Poughkeepsie
Who enjoyed getting just a little **tipsy**
One night he drank enough
To make perception tough
And wound up trying to sleep with a pixie
(He had gone a little too far admits he)

2
There was a sweet gal named Mitzie
Who favored bars that were ritzy
Sam picked her up at the bar
But he did not get very far
For she was drunk not just a little **tipsy**

329. METAL - 14 MAY 2022

1
A rare stable **metal** is tantalum
The rarest is actually francium
Which has no practical use
It's too unstable and loose
Most women prefer rings of platinum

2
The story of Hansel and Gretel
Is one that did me unsettle
If the witch's small oven
Was owned by a coven*
They would have been cooked in a **metal** kettle
(When they escaped they put pedal to the **metal**)

330. YIELD - 15 MAY 2022

At the stop sign he failed to **yield**
After that his fate was sealed
When he received a ticket
He claimed that's not cricket
But in court he never appealed

331. DELVE - 16 MAY 2022

1
I did not want to **delve** too deeply
So at first I probed only meekly
Shocked by what I did uncover
My wife had found a new lover
Now I wonder if she's planning to keep me

2

I knew there were exactly twelve
To remember all I would have to **delve**
Recalling each would be ambitious
All the Twelve Days of Christmas*
If I fail to the performance I will shelve
(I bet the days don't' even remember themselve)

332. BEING - 17 MAY 2022

1

The old adage to be or not to be
Is about **being** or not **being** you see
Well if Hamlet is so distressed
And so severely depressed
He needs to learn how to ski
(Or go to college and get a degree)
(Although of happiness there is no guarantee)

2

The church's 14th century decreeings*
Is the reason we are called human **being**s
We could never be ignored
Made in the image of the lord
Thereby our special status guaranteeing
(Though some are still disagreeing)

333. SCOUR - 18 MAY 2022

Aladdin's disposition was dour
So a dull lamp he decided to **scour**
Suddenly out of his lamp
Popped a Genie a scamp
For each wish he charged ten dollars an hour
(Poor Aladdin was pulled in by his power)
(The poor boy really only needed a shower)

334. GLASS - 19 MAY 2022

1
Some consider the music of Phillip **Glass***
A bit of a musical morass
His style is minimalistic
While others think it stylistic
For he never employs any brass
(The repetition suggests he's at an impasse)

2
Start with quartz or silica to make **glass***
Quite different than making brass
Don't forget the limestone
Whether floated or blown
And finally add soda ash
(Not too much now just a dash)

335. GAMER - 20 MAY 2022

I became addicted to video games
So I lost all interest in dames
Upon becoming a **gamer**
I became much saner
For it increased the gray matter of my brain*

336. SCRAP - 21 MAY 2022

I always gave my dog **scrap**s from my plate
Which of course he always gladly ate
No matter how many I gave
Fido continued to crave
If I stopped he'd become so irate
(His appetite I never could sate)
(He eventually became overweight)

337. MONEY - 22 MAY 2022

1

Before **money** everyone everywhere bartered
With the Mesopotamian shekel it started
Using silver or gold
Goods were bought and sold
Now financial transactions are credit carded
(Now all of my movements are charted)

2

The prediction was right on the **money**
If it came to be it would not be funny
For it seemed quite remote
For Biden so many would vote
Allowing our country to be run by a dummy

338. HINGE - 23 MAY 2022

My prognosis on a blood test did **hinge**
So I allowed them to use a syringe
When I extended my arm
It was with some alarm
That I felt an unbearable twinge
(On my golf game this did impinge)
(After which I went on a binge)

339. ALBUM - 24 MAY 2022
See 144(1) GROUP

While drinking a bottle of Macallan
We listened to the latest Beatles **album**
Lucy in the Sky
Made us feel high
For this record was such an amalgam

340. VOUCH - 25 MAY 2022

He spent all his days on the couch
For he was such a complete slouch
Smoking marijuana
Seeking nirvana
For his character no one would **vouch**
(It didn't help that he was such a grouch)

341. ASSET - 26 MAY 2022

There was a gold digger from Manhasset
Who for a rich man had a trap set
She had a marvelous behind
But her intelligence he did find
Was far from her greatest **asset**
(That he didn't mind was tacit)

342. TIARA - 27 MAY 2022

1
A woman by the name of Tamara
Really loved to wear a **tiara**
She wore it to a lagoon
And was peed on by a racoon
Now she is sick with a Leptospira*

2
The distinction between a **tiara** and crown
Either one must be worn with a gown
Tiaras go halfway around the head
And unless I've been misled
A crown goes completely around
(This knowledge is truly profound)

343. CREPT - 28 MAY 2022

1
While I peacefully slept
Into my bed quietly **crept**
The womanizer Casanova*
Who tried to roll me over
But he proved not to be that adept
(So out of my bed I leapt)

2
While she peacefully slept
Into her bed he **crept**
Her faithful dog Rover
Who rolled her over
But she never knew for she overslept

344. BAYOU - 29 MAY 2022

1
It was in a **bayou** of Louisiana
That I learned Cajun* grammar
From French Acadians
Who became Canadians
Their lingo will make you stammer

French Canadians traveled to Louisiana
Never reaching the edge of Alabama
Where they mated in caves
And **bayou**s with Negro slaves
Resulting in mysterious Creole* arcana

2
I once knew a guy who
Moved to a southern **bayou**
I heard a year later
He got eaten by an alligator
He's the one person I never said goodbye to

345. ATOLL - 30 MAY 2022

1
My ship sank in a typhoon
On a Pacific **atoll** I did maroon
Just like Robinson Crusoe*
Of whom you may know
It would be a while until I found a saloon
(Right now I need to fight this raccoon)

2
An **atoll** is made of beautiful coral
About this there's no need to quarrel
A reef surrounded by a lagoon
On which seashells are strewn
Except for palm trees there not much that's floral
(To this limerick there's no moral)

346. MANOR - 31 MAY 2022

Tarzan was the king of the apes
Lost in the jungle when a neonate
Lord of the **manor** father Greystoke*
In the jungle sadly did croak
But the child survived make no mistake

He was raised on zebra and hippo steaks
He also enjoyed elephant crepes
He loved crocodile tail
But refused to eat kale
His favorite food was sauteed snakes

With this really excellent diet
He developed a voice not so quiet
His high-pitched iconic yell
Through the jungle traveled well
If you don't believe me go ahead and try it

One lucky day he ran into Jane
His desire he was unable contain
So he swung her with great ease
To his **manor** house in the trees
Which was originally Cheeta's domain
(And there they did happily remain)
(To this day he's never been on a train)

347. CREAK - 1 JUNE 2022

1
Through the hallway I did sneak
To her door's keyhole to peek
So she wouldn't know
I walked slowly on tip toe
But she found out for the floorboards did **creak**
(I really am a bit of a freak)

2
I really should have known
I would have a **creak**y bone
It's the arthritis I fear
Everyone will hear
My anguished moan and groan
(Aging I do not condone)

348. SHOWY - 2 JUNE 2022

1
An extroverted chap named Joey
Was quite ostentatiously **showy**
Downhill skiers did dread
When he was skiing ahead
Especially when it was snowy

2

It was quite a **showy** display
An attempt to avoid turning gray
When she dyed her hair green
She looked quite obscene
And in complete disarray
(She is in a state of dismay)
(I think she looks okay)

349. PHASE - 3 JUNE 2022

1

I love observing each **phase** of the moon
Women's menstrual cycles are often in tune
The waxing and waning
Requires some explaining
A full moon makes stargazing inopportune
(To the high tides no one is immune)

2

It is just another passing **phase**
When he doesn't get his ways
It's unclear where it came from
His powerful temper tantrum
This kid is just so difficult to raise
(I swear I want to leave him in a maze)

350. FROTH - 4 JUNE 2022

1

He was concerned that his urine did **froth**
It looked quite a lot like broth
Did he have porphyria*
Or was it proteinuria*
He would worry about this thenceforth

2
A biology teacher named Roth
Wondered what made beer **froth**
CO_2 bubbles rise to the top
Forming a head from protein and hops
We learned from what the Sumerians* doth
(In it you might find floating a moth)

351. DEPTH - 5 JUNE 2022

36,000 feet the greatest **depth** of any ocean
Deeper than Mt Everest is tall what a notion
The great Mariana Trench*
The Pacific does quench
This thought fills me with deep emotion
(Thinking about it sets me in motion)

352. GLOOM - 6 JUNE 2022

1
A cloud of **gloom** descended upon the city
Coal smokestacks made the air gritty
An temperature inversion
Produced a pea soup fog immersion
For a week life in London was shitty*
(About it I'm sure someone sings a ditty)

2
It was a foggy night with the darkest **gloom**
I felt an awkward sense of impending doom
I am a grave robber
A profession macabre
In the graveyard I will open a tomb
(For anatomical dissection I presume)
(For medical students this will be a boon)

353. FLOOD - 7 JUNE 2022

1

It was a worldwide antediluvian **flood**
Submerging all in an alluvial mud
Earth was deluged and dark
Thank God for Noah's ark
Without it the world's end had been adjudged
(Do you think God in his wrath may have misjudged?)

2

New Orleans was completely inundated
Hurricane Katrina* left it devastated
Levees broke causing a **flood**
Triggering mud and spilled blood
The costliest tropical cyclone it is rated
(Many homes were left vacated)

354. TRAIT - 8 JUNE 2022

1

It must have been a genetic **trait**
That verbs she could not conjugate
Yet she couldn't be brighter
And became a famous writer
Whom no one could ever translate
(Reading her triggers feisty debate)

2

There was a young woman named Kate
Who loved to stay up so very late
She never arose* before noon
Couldn't be aroused* in the afternoon
For being nocturnal was an inherent **trait**
(Her addiction to caffeine we cannot negate)

355. GIRTH - 9 JUNE 2022
See 386 BERTH

Have you ever wondered about the earth
What might be its equatorial **girth***
The miles between each pole
Times pi achieves that goal
This knowledge has genuine worth
(This limerick is useful but has no mirth)

356. PIETY - 10 JUNE 2022

There are many forms or variety
Of expression of ones' **piety**
Never drink too much
Or a woman's ass touch
That would be an outrageous impropriety
(One must always maintain their sobriety)
(That will spare you unwanted notoriety)

357. GOOSE - 11 JUNE 2022
See 358(1) FLOAT

1
Howard Hughes manufactured the Spruce **Goose***
Which was a very difficult thing to produce
Known as the flying boat
Almost too big to float
Too cumbersome to be put to any use
(And it had one heck of a caboose)

2
An ornithologist tried to induce
His fowls to strangely reproduce
He crossed a chicken with a duck
And with a crazy bit of luck
He wound up with a quacking **goose**
(He decided to name it Toulouse)

358. FLOAT - 12 JUNE 2022
See 357(1) GOOSE

1

His principle Archimedes* did promote
Explaining why objects sink or **float**
Free of flamboyancy
He called it buoyancy
It explained why a boat stays a**float**
(His concept was worthy of note)

2

I never ever intended to gloat
About the woman on whom I dote
She won't give me the time of day
For fear I might lead her astray
But that is exactly what **float**s my boat

359. DONOR - 13 JUNE 2022
See 247(1) OTHER 307 PLANT 390(1) LIVER for 359(2)

1

Marilyn was a real sad loner
Ever since I had known her
She suffered from Agoraphobia*
So she never attended symposia
When she died she became a liver **donor**
(There was nobody to bemoan her)

2

An ancient Greek poet named Homer
Developed a lymphosarcoma
Hippocrates* treated him
But much to his chagrin
Homer died for lack of a **donor**
(He died without to his name a single kronor)

360. ATONE - 14 JUNE 2022

There was once a gangster Al Capone*
A crime boss whose reputation had grown
Until one day such a pity
The stool pigeon Frank Nitty
Squealed in order to **atone**

Forced to **atone** in the Alcatraz prison
Where symptoms of paresis had arisen
Something was amiss
Capone had neurosyphilis*
Because he never underwent circumcision*
(I wonder if he regretted his decision)

361. PRIMO - 15 JUNE 2022

There once was a man named Nino
Who had ten sibs as far as we know
He was born first
A dog or two was interspersed
But in his family he was the **primo**
(I hear these days he's into emo*)

362. APRON - 16 JUNE 2022

1
There once was a confused elderly matron
Who never cooked without wearing an **apron**
For should the grease splatter
She would flee and scatter
And never finish frying the bacon
(She said she's still rather shaken)

2
Sue wore an **apron** when answering the door
Only that and absolutely nothing more
Cooking for her new beau
She was all aglow
Making it easy her body to explore
(He couldn't wait so they did it on the floor)
(The neighbors did their best to ignore)

363. BLOWN - 17 JUNE 2022

1
Murano island is a place in Venice
The glass **blown** there is not Lennox
Does one in beauty the other surpass
Murano is the most beautiful **blown** glass
That opinion is by uniform consensus

2
A great opportunity he had **blown**
It was an error for him to postpone
Immediate evacuation
From his tropical island location
Soon he'll be hit by a powerful cyclone
(He stayed to find his cologne)

364. CACAO - 18 JUNE 2022

Chocolate is made from the **cacao** bean
And it contains theobromine
What's **cacao*** and cocoa
Does anybody really know
The bean's the same there's nothing in between

But if the **cacao** bean is processed
And out of it the butter is pressed
The remainder is cocoa powder
I cannot say this any louder
Cacao is sugar free and is healthiest
(Sorry for a moment I was possessed)
(I'm so glad we have this addressed)

365. LOSER - 19 JUNE 2022

I never intended to choose her
She was a disgraceful boozer
I guess she chose me
For it was clear to see
That I was a complete **loser**
(Will I ever be able to lose her)

366. INPUT - 20 JUNE 2022

All of our visual **input**
Gets interpreted in our cerebral occiput*
At the rear of our brain
Our visual domain
If it's working nothing gets overlooked
(How many fingers am I holding crooked?)

367. GLOAT - 21 JUNE 2022

I certainly did not mean to **gloat**
Nor violence do I wish to promote
When he insulted me
After interrupting me
I grabbed him by his skinny throat
(Please don't put that in a quote)

368. AWFUL - 22 JUNE 2022

1

There was once an unfortunate toad
Who while hopping on a country road
Was stopped dead in its tracks
By a series of **awful** attacks
From a parasitic nematode*
(You'd think they'd have some moral code)

2

I created an **awful** mess
No one expected any less
I came in last in the race
Which was a disgrace
But at least I was making progress

369. BRINK - 23 JUNE 2022

See 21(1) DEATH 382 FLUFF for 369(2)

1

The world was at the **brink** of war
Nuclear missiles placed off Florida's shore
For the Cuban missile crisis*
Involved nuclear devices
We were closer to the **brink** than ever before
(This terrified me down to my core)

2

Just like in act 5 scene 8 of Macbeth
I was at the very **brink** of death
For I could not flee
When you drew close to me
I almost died from the smell of your breath

370. SMITE - 24 JUNE 2022

It was during the Jews' biblical plight
The lord promised Moses he would invite
Egypt's Pharaoh
To let his people go
Or he would **smite** them with all of his might

So God brought to Egypt ten plagues*
To force Pharaoh to free the Jewish slaves
The last plague was the worst
Death of Egyptian children born first
The lord did **smite** them in deadly waves
(Left behind so many devastating graves)

371. BEADY - 25 JUNE 2022

His eyes were gray and rather **beady**
He had the air of one who's greedy
When he shot and killed
My aunt Mathilde
I prayed his arrest would be speedy

372. RUSTY - 26 JUNE 2022

1
Her figure was rotund and busty
She was provocative and lusty
She acted high class
Ignoring my pass
It looks like I'm really getting **rusty**
(She must have considered me fusty)

2
I accidentally stepped on a **rusty** nail
Which caused me to moan and to wail
My concern over tetanus
Made me feel onerous
So to the ER I quickly beat a trail

373. RETRO - 27 JUNE 2022

They say a **retro** style of dress
Could make you look like a mess
Wearing clothes in style again
From a decade that has been
It's your parents you are trying to impress
(The bell bottoms look rather good I confess)

374. DROLL - 28 JUNE 2022

His sense of humor was always **droll**
And on his victims it took a toll
For he was sarcastic
Bombastic and iconoclastic
In other words a complete asshole
(Not one of them did he try to console)

375. GAWKY - 29 JUNE 2022

In addition to his acne he was **gawky**
His voice was high pitched and squawky
A typical preteen
Somewhat unclean
With a complexion pale and chalky
(Time to move back to Milwaukee)

376. HUTCH - 30 JUNE 2022

Mother kept her best dishware in a **hutch**
The children were never allowed to touch
Although this fact is rather minor
China was porcelain's first designer
Marco Polo brought it to Europe and the Dutch
(Never try to use it for a crutch)

377. PINTO - 1 JULY 2022

According to my many reliable sources
The word **pinto** describes beans and horses
Both are speckled or spotted
Only horses can be trotted
Beans are served in many more courses
(Beans are much more common as food sources)

378. EGRET - 2 JULY 2022

See 151 HERON

It seems I always do forget
How to properly pronounce **egret**
So I refer to them as herons
For they have the same operons*
I don't think that will make them upset
(If it does I hold the highest regret)

379. LILAC - 3 JULY 2022

It happened a long while back
This charming fellow named Isaak
Was completely overpowered
By a gorgeous purple flower
Not a pansy but a **lilac**

Their purple color so divine
I now take the liberty to opine
Is the most beautiful floral
Seen in phenomena auroral
In a bouquet **lilac**'s beauty will shine
(The bias here is clearly mine)

380. SEVER - 4 JULY 2022

See 169(1) USHER 317(1) STORY for 380(1)

1

I am trying quite hard to **sever**
My attachment to you forever
For unlike Annabel Lee*
You're not buried by the sea
But alive and in love with Trevor
(I don't see the appeal whatsoever)

2

The buzzsaw **severed** all of my fingers
The memory of that day still lingers
Now to pick my nose
I employ all my toes
All five on each foot are dead ringers

381. FIELD - 5 JULY 2022

1

Farmer Claud's fertile **field**
Produced corn with copious yield
That he fed to his swine
The pigs thought it divine
For it caused them to oink and to squeal

2
Biden's press secretary is well heeled
Difficult questions she's required to **field**
Karine Jean-Pierre
For the truth doesn't care
The real facts always remain concealed
(At some point they will be revealed)

382. FLUFF - 6 JULY 2022

See 21(1) DEATH 369(2) BRINK

The Thane of Fife known as Lord MacDuff
In Shakespeare's play MacBeth's life did snuff
For he committed regicide
A deed that he denied
Or did his lines the forgetful actor **fluff**
(Needless to say this killer did not bluff)

383. AGAPE - 7 JULY 2022

1
In Africa among the great apes
I stood with my mouth **agape**
At how these primates did savor
Licentious promiscuous behavior
While never bothering to undrape
(Look is that one eating a grape)

2
I stood there **agape** and in wonder
Trying hard not to commit a blunder
After she took off her clothes
With her private parts exposed
She laid back with her legs asunder
(How could I ever have shunned her)

384. VOICE - 8 JULY 2022
See 253 CHANT for 384(2)

1
I now always do rejoice
Every time I hear his **voice**
My name is Patty
He's my sugar daddy
And he's given me a brand-new Rolls Royce
(I'd have preferred a Mustang given the choice)

2
I am often told I have a deep **voice**
About that I never had a choice
In church choir I sing bass
Although I feel out of place
You see my first name is Joyce
(Now I have to sing with the boys)

385. STEAD - 9 JULY 2022
See 398 TRYST

One day a rumor I did spread
That I was just terrific in bed
I swear I wasn't bragging
My romantic trysts were flagging
I hoped that this would stand me in good **stead**
(I hope no one thinks I've misled)

386. BERTH - 10 JULY 2022
See 355 GIRTH

I needed to give him a wide **berth**
But could not due to his great girth*
At four hundred pound
He was incredibly round
His waist seemed as big as the earth
(Wonder how his mother felt at his birth)

387. MADAM - 11 JULY 2022
See 251(1) VIVID 298(2) CHUNK for 387(1)

1
In the garden of Eden lay Adam*
Contentedly stroking his **madam**
And loud was his mirth
For on all of the earth
There were only two balls and he had 'em

2
She ran a house of ill repute
Employing gals that were quite cute
Free of venereal disease
Whose aim was to please
Madam X was awfully astute
(Wonder if she needs a recruit)

388. NIGHT - 12 JULY 2022

1
I am regularly considered a **night** owl
It's quite late when I throw in the towel
Night owls have a higher IQ
But more diabetes type 2
So I'm not sure if I should smile or scowl
(Sometimes I am tempted to howl)
(I'm not a werewolf there is nothing afoul)
(Don't mind me I'm just out on the prowl)

2
When the sun sinks out of sight
Shortly later day turns to **night**
Nocturnal animals hunt and peep
Diurnal ones curl up to sleep
That reverses at dawn's early light

389. BLAND - 13 JULY 2022

1

The fondue offered is rather **bland**
Yet it is always in high demand
For the diners never knew better
Instead of Gruyére they used Cheddar
Something I could never understand
(I really think they're being scammed)

2

She gazed at me with a **bland** smile
Perhaps it was just her style
For her true feelings for me
With her expression failed to agree
Deep down she was completely hostile
(But maybe that's just while we're on trial)

390. LIVER - 14 JULY 2022

See 247(1) OTHER 307 PLANT 359(1+2) DONOR

1

I doubt I could ever come to forgive her
She refused to donate part of her **liver**
I needed a transplant
But she said I just can't
Now it's clear I can never outlive her
(At the thought of this I do shiver)

2

An organ you can't overrate
Livers found only in vertebrates
Without one you can't get by
For poisons you must detoxify
And it's so great it can regenerate
(I don't have to think about it this is innate)

391. WEDGE - 15 JULY 2022

1
While flying time and time again
I get seated between two fat men
While **wedge**d between them
I don't wish to demean them
But for more space I have a great yen

2
There was a rude prankster named Reggie
Who loved to give his classmates a **wedg**ie
But he pulled too tight
Which just wasn't right
When behind you he always made you edgy

392. ROOMY - 16 JULY 2022

I once arranged for a prostitute to do me
But I found her vagina too **roomy**
So I refused to pay
After a brief delay
I did so because she blew me
(Her skills really threw me)

393. WACKY - 17 JULY 2022

My idea was completely **wacky**
At first it also seemed tacky
I adopted a pet rock
No one thought this was a crock
So I decided to name it Jackie
(Now it is my faithful lackey)

394. FLOCK - 18 JULY 2022

See 166(1) CHEAT for 394(2)

1

Is it a **flock** or a herd
It's a **flock** for some animals and every bird
Never say a herd of birds
That rhymes but it's absurd
The silliest thing that I have ever heard
(You can never win with the wrong word)
(Either way I'm sure the bird will not be deterred)

2

He was preaching to the **flock**
The congregation was in shock
Claiming there were several
Active forms of the devil
But that was just a bunch of schlock*
(Of your biases take stock)

395. ANGRY - 19 JULY 2022

1

He was an **angry** young man
An illegal alien from Sudan
He came as a terrorist
An explosives specialist
To blow up the pentagon was his plan
(He took the wrong plane and ended up in Japan)

2

Do you wonder how it all began
The expression **angry** young man
From the play Look Back in Anger*
Which detailed middle class rancor
Later a movie which made it to Cannes

396. TRITE - 20 JULY 2022

Her arguments were becoming so **trite**
Claiming it was her personal birthright
To talk temperature in Centigrade
But she was unable to dissuade
My preference to use Fahrenheit
(Others prefer Kelvin that's right)

397. APHID - 21 JULY 2022
See 399 MIDGE

A small soft-bodied insect the **aphid**
Lives upon the crops you have planted
So spray your plants with water
More on leaves that are broader
Before feeding them to your pet squid
(I hear they're a fan of salad)

398. TRYST - 22 JULY 2022
See 385 STEAD

I once had a **tryst** with Tristan*
A very handsome young man
When we drank a love potion
We were overpowered with emotion
Of love then the trouble began
(For Isolde that wasn't the plan)

399. MIDGE - 23 JULY 2022*

See 279(2) DEPOT 397 APHID

A bite from an aphid **midge*** if you please
Fortunately carries no harmful disease
But a bite from a mosquito
Carries many you may know
Malaria Dengue Encephalitis Japanese
(Don't be afraid to slap them or give them a squeeze)

400. POWER - 24 JULY 2022

1
4 is the **power** of 2
This is something I thought you knew
But the power of 3
Between you and me
I can't even begin to tell you
(Don't ask when this homework is due)

2
The transfer of **power** must be peaceful
Never ever should it be deceitful
With the assassination of Kennedy
Lyndon Johnson took over to remedy
Yet at that time the nation was fearful
(The response to his death was tearful)

FOOTNOTES TO SELECT WORDLE LIMERICKS

A footnote on the footnotes:

Some limericks are clear in their traditional off-colored nature and do not require explanation. Others are more complicated but the limerick itself, despite the limitations of only 5 lines within which to elaborate, is in of itself sufficient to relate the intended information. Others still, such as the assassination of President John F. Kennedy, are so well known generally that, again, no further explanation is needed. There are, however, a substantial number of my Wordle Limericks that have more obscure references, require further explanation or present opportunities to educate. It is for this last group that footnotes are provided.

The footnotes are intended to be brief but sufficient in making the meaning of the limerick clear by providing concise background information. The majority of these footnotes are obtained from Wikipedia but many other sources have been utilized as well.

In the footnotes, some limericks will make reference to other related limericks. This is denoted by the limerick number and the number within the limericks if there is more than one. For example, limerick #21(1) DEATH has within it references to limerick #369(2) BRINK. This informs the reader that the 2nd limerick for the word BRINK contains a related subject to limerick 21(1) DEATH. In this case, they both contain references to Macbeth and death.

A spreadsheet that lists chronologically the daily Wordle words that triggers the limericks and provides information on the number of limericks for each word, the numbers of other limericks dealing with a related subject, and provides numbers representing the category of subject matter for each limerick (of which there are 33 categories). An alphabetical list of categories are listed preceding the limerick section. An alphabetical listing of the Wordle words is provided in a second table as well.

#0 CIGAR
*The Lewinsky scandal refers to the sexual relationship between president Bill Clinton and young White House intern, Monica Lewinsky, in the mid to late 1990s. He stated that he did not, in fact, have sexual relations with her in a televised announcement in 1998 but was found culpable after investigation into his actions. This led directly to his impeachment; the second in presidential history, preceded by Andrew Johnson and followed by Donald Trump's two impeachments.

See #290 NATAL

#1 REBUT

*King Tut, also known as Tutankhamun (1341 BC-1323 BC), was a pharaoh of the Eighteenth Dynasty of ancient Egypt. He reigned from the age of nine to nineteen and was worshipped as a deity throughout his rule. The discovery of his tomb in 1922 remains one of the most monumental archeological discoveries of all time.

See #35(2) PAPER

#3 HUMPH

*A golem is an animated anthropomorphic creature made of clay or dust, brought to life through rites in Jewish folklore. The name comes from the Hebrew word "golem", referring to something incomplete or unfinished.

See #87 GOLEM

#7 EVADE

*Genghis Khan (1162-1227) was one of the most famous conquerors in history. He brought all of the nomadic tribes of Mongolia under his disciplinary military state and then proceeded to stretch his reign out in all directions, creating the great Mongol Empire: the largest land empire in history.

See #169(1) USHER

#11 DWARF

*Somatotype is a theory proposed in the 1940s by American psychologist and eugenicist William Herbert Sheldon (1898-1977) to categorize the human physique, which he called somatotypes: ectomorph, mesomorph and endomorph. An ectomorph is skinny, weak, usually tall, intelligent, introverted and anxious. A mesomorph is strong, muscular, thick, competitive, extroverted and tough. An endomorph is fat, short, outgoing, friendly, happy and laid-back. This stereotyping, although popular in the 1950s, has since been dismissed as quackery.

See #101 SALAD

#16 QUIET

*All Quiet on the Western Front (published 1929) was written by a German veteran of World War I, Erich Maria Remarque (1898-1970). It is about a German soldiers' trauma, both physical and psychological, during the war as well as after. It is an anti-war and pacifist novel which led to it being banned in Italy and resulted in the revocation of Remarque's German citizenship and his subsequent exile.

#18 ABATE

*Hyperphagia refers to an extreme, insatiable hunger. It is often connected to diabetes or other medical issues, such as hyperthyroidism or atypical depression.

*An endocrinologist is a physician who specializes in conditions related to hormones.

See #45 CRATE #110 ABACK

#21 DEATH

*Also known as "The Scottish Play", *Macbeth* is a tragedy written by William Shakespeare (1564-1616). It is a tale of political power and manipulation, (told by an idiot, full of sound and fury, signifying nothing). The "tomorrow, tomorrow, and tomorrow" is from Macbeth's soliloquy, triggered by his learning of Lady Macbeth's death.

*The Grim Reaper is a representation of death, embodied by a skeleton in a black robe, holding a scythe.

*Thanatos is the personification of death in Greek mythology. He appeared when the three Fates snipped a human's string of life (thus ending it) to bring them to the Underworld.

*The Battle of the Alamo (February 16th to March 6th, 1836) was a desperate battle between Mexicans and Texans in which every single Texan defender died, including Davy Crockett and Jim Bowie. It occurred in a historic Spanish mission and fortress compound in what is now San Antonio.

See #369(2) BRINK #382 FLUFF for #21(1)

#23 CRUST

*Alexander Fleming (1881-1955), a Scottish physician, is known for accidentally discovering that the mold on an abandoned petri dish prevented the bacteria on the dish from growing. Through this, he discovered penicillin which has saved billions of lives.

*"Another one bites the dust" is an idiomatic expression that typically refers to someone dying, a failure in a contest or game, or that something has stopped existing or failed. The phrase has been around since (at least) 1750 and was popularized by the American Western movies (1930s), in which characters were thrown from their horses to the dusty ground.

#24 STOOL

*Scatology is the biologically oriented study of excrement for either taxonomic purposes or the study of prehistoric diets. It also refers to interest in obscene matters, especially in literature.

#29 BATTY

*"Meshuga" is Yiddish for "crazy".

#30 PRIDE

*derivative*Pride and Prejudice* is an 1813 novel written by Jane Austen (1775-1817). The novel follows the character development of Elizabeth Bennet, a critical and intelligent protagonist who experiences the repercussions of hasty judgment. It is a love story as well as a reflection of the classism and culture of the era. Elizabeth and Mr. Darcy must both overcome their biases in order to understand each other and, eventually, love each other.

   See #159(2) WROTE for #30(2)

#31 FLOSS
   *"Edentulous" means "lacking in teeth".

#32 HELIX
   *Watson and Crick were the scientists responsible for the discovery of the double helical structure of DNA in 1951-53, for which they received a Nobel Prize in Medicine in 1962.

#35 PAPER
   *The Egyptians invented the pictorial script referred to as hieroglyphics in 3000 BC, marking the beginning of their civilization. Today, any writing system employing images as symbols for various semantic entities, rather than the abstract signs used in alphabets, is referred to as hieroglyphics. Jean-Francois Champollion (1790-1832), a French linguist, deciphered the Rosetta Stone and cracked the hieroglyphic code.

   See #1 REBUT for #35(2)

#37 WHELP
   See #90 ROUND

#39 OUTDO
   *The Sioux Indians are a confederacy of several tribes that speak three different dialects: the Lakota, Dakota and Nakota. Their original homelands were in what is now Wisconsin, Minnesota, and North and South Dakota.

   See #57 STAND for #39(2)

#40 ADOBE
   *Adobe is a mixture of clay, sand and silt that dries into a hard uniform mass and makes sun dried bricks used for building.
   *The Gobi Desert is a vast, arid region in northern China and southern Mongolia.

#41 CRAZY
   *Edison and Tesla were involved in the War of the Currents in the late 1880s, with Edison promoting the use of direct current (DC) for power distribution, for which he held the patents. Tesla

supported alternating current (AC) as it allowed larger quantities of energy to be transmitted to power large cities.

#42 SOWER

*Dante Alighieri (1265-1321) was an Italian poet, writer and philosopher. His *Divine Comedy* is widely considered one of the most important poems of the Middle Ages and the greatest literary work in the Italian language. He is credited for establishing the use of the vernacular in literature at a time when most poetry was written in Latin, and was accessible only to educated readers.

*In *Dante's Inferno*, written in 1314, there are 9 circles of hell. They are in descending order, with the deeper levels representing a greater degree of sin and punishment: First Circle: Limbo, Second Circle: Lust, Third Circle: Gluttony, Fourth Circle: Greed, Fifth Circle: Anger, Sixth Circle: Heresy, Seventh Circle: Violence, Eight Circle: Fraud, Ninth Circle: Treachery. The Sowers of Discord would fit into Circle 6, while the bull thrower doesn't fit perfectly into any circle. The torture of those souls in the lowest circle is not waterboarding. This deepest level of Dante's hell is a frozen wasteland occupied by history's greatest traitors.

#45 CRATE

*Did you ever wonder why goods sent by truck are called 'ship'ments but goods sent by ships are called 'car'go?

See #18 ABATE #110 ABACK

#46 CLUCK

*A schmuck is a stupid, foolish or unlikable person. It is derived from the Yiddish "shmok", literally: "penis".

#47 SPIKE

*Dwight David Eisenhower (1890-1969) was an American military officer and statesman who served as the 34th president of the United States from 1953 to 1961. During World War II, he was Supreme Commander of the Allied Expeditionary Force in Europe and achieved the 5 star rank as general of the army.

*POTUS is an acronym for the president of the United States, often used as a nickname.

#49 POUND

*EU stands for "European Union" which is a supranational political and economic union of 27 member states that are primarily located in Europe. The population is 447 million.

*Brexit is an abbreviation of two words: "Britain" and "exit". It refers to the withdrawal of the United Kingdom (UK) from the European Union on January 31, 2020. The U.K. is the only sovereign country to have left the EU.

*A navel orange has a small belly-button-like appendage at the apex where it is cut from the tree during harvesting. It is called as such because it resembles a human "outie" belly button.

#51 LINEN

*A spinster is a woman whose occupation is to spin thread and yarn. It is used today to refer to an unmarried woman who is unlikely to marry. In colonial times, families depended on the income generated by the daughter who spun fiber into cloth and therefore they were rarely permitted to marry.

*"Can't put a pin in" means you cannot easily identify or pinpoint a specific grammatical error in a sentence or piece of writing.

See #216 PRICK

#54 BOOBY

See #271 MOVIE for #54(2)

#56 FIRST

William Randolph Hurst Sr. (1863-1951) was an American businessman, newspaper publisher, and politician who developed the nation's largest newspaper chain and media company. In 1941, Orson Welles (1915-1985) released the movie *Citizen Kane*, which told the story of a rags to riches rise by Charles Foster Kane, a fictional person whose life is based on Hurst. The film proved to be a financial failure despite its artistic success because Hurst blocked its release to the many theaters he controlled through his media enterprises.

#57 STAND

*The Battle of the Little Bighorn (June 25-26, 1876) marked the most decisive Native American victory and worst U.S. Army defeat in the Plains Indian War. No U.S. Army soldiers survived the battle, including Custer.

*George Armstrong Custer (1839-1876) was a United states Army officer and cavalry commander in the American Civil War and the American Indian Wars.

See #39(2) OUTDO

#58 BELLY

See #103 SPICY

#59 IVORY

*The white piano keys were originally ivory from elephant tusks, used for its hard-wearing and durable nature. However, piano manufacturers stopped using ivory in 1956. Asian and European brands ceased production of ivory keytops in the mid 1980s.

#61 PRINT

*Gustav Klimt (1862-1918) was an Austrian symbolist artist noted for his paintings, murals and sketches. His primary subject was the female body and his works are marked by frank eroticism.

#63 DRAIN

*The direction of the spin of water going down a drain is theoretically different in the southern hemisphere from the northern hemisphere due to the Coriolis effect, which is caused by the rotation of the earth. It produces an effect that tends to accelerate draining water in a clockwise direction in the northern hemisphere and counterclockwise in the southern. The Coriolis effect is real but a bathtub, toilet or sink is not large enough for this effect to be observable.

*The last line is a reference to the song "Ain't That A Shame" by Fats Domino, released in 1955. See footnote for #300 SHAME.

#64 BRIBE

*"Hygrocybe" is a genus of gilled fungi.

#66 PANEL

*See #201 BANAL

#68 FLUME

*A flume is a raised channel used to transport water from a source (such as a river), to the top of a water wheel. The water flow is directed onto the blade of the wheel causing it to rotate. Flumes were used for various purposes, namely transportation for electricity and logs.

#69 OFFAL

*"Offal" was originally named after garbage or the part of the animal that would fall off when butchered. This consists of the internal organs of the animal (innards), some of which are frequently consumed. Today the liver, kidneys, stomach (tripe), pancreas and thymus (sweetbreads) are consumed frequently while other organs such as lung and brain rarely are.

*"Dreck" is Yiddish for "rubbish" or "trash".

#73 ARGUE

*The second limerick is not original, but is so good that I don't believe I could do better. I am including it because it is simply too good not to. It is from William S. Baring-Gould's *The Lure of the Limerick* (New York: Clarkson N. Potter, 1967).

#74 BLEED

*Hemophilia B is a hereditary bleeding disorder caused by a deficiency of blood clotting factor IX. The more common hereditary Hemophilia A is due to a deficiency of factor VIII. Hemophilia B was known as the Royal Disease because so many descendants of the intermarried royal families of Europe suffered from it (carried by the females; the inheritance is sex-linked). Rasputin (1869-1916), a peasant who proclaimed himself a healer with the ability to predict the future, won the favor of Czar Nicholas II and Czarina Alexandra through his ability to stop the bleeding of their hemophiliac son Alexei Nikolaevich (1904-1918). In doing so, he garnered influence over the royal family and the affairs of state, but outside of the court, he was licentious and highly sexual, using his power to seduce many women (despite being married). He earned the surname "Rasputin", which translates to "debauched one" in Russian.

See #180 USING

#75 DELTA
*The delta symbol (Δ) often represents change, particularly in calculus: the mathematical study of change.

#77 TOTEM
*Odin is the Norse god of war and death. Today, he is most known as a character in the Marvel comic books, and more recently in movies of the Marvel Cinematic Universe.

#83 LAPEL
See #257(2) MOURN

#84 START
See #158 RETCH for 84(1)

#87 GOLEM
*A "slalom" is a ski race down a winding course marked by flags or poles.
*See footnote to #3 HUMPH for an explanation of the Golem.

See #3 GOLEM

#89 LOOPY
*Kabuki is a popular and traditional Japanese drama format, performed with highly stylized singing and dancing.

#90 ROUND
*The Hound of the Baskervilles is the third of four crime novels by Sir Arthur Conan Doyle featuring Sherlock Holmes.

See #37 WHELP

#93 GAMMA
*The third letter in the Greek alphabet is gamma (γ).
*Gamma rays have the shortest wavelength and greatest energy of any wave in the electromagnetic spectrum. These rays are the most harmful external hazard. Gamma rays and X-rays can pass through a person damaging cells in their path. Gamma ray bursts are the most powerful thing in the universe.

See #277(1) PURGE for #93(1)
See #160(1) CLOCK #179(1) TRACE for #93(2)

#94 LABOR
*A tabor is a small drum.

#95 ISLET
*The islets of Langerhans are groups of cells located throughout the pancreas. They secrete insulin and glucagon, hormones that regulate glucose metabolism.

#96 CIVIC
*Rudolph William Guiliani (b. 1944) is an American lawyer and politician who served as the 107th mayor of New York City, from 1994 to 2001. Under his leadership rampant crime was brought under control and his adept handling of the city after the 9/11 terrorist attacks in 2001 resulted in the moniker "America's Mayor". He was named Time Magazine's person of the year in 2001.

#97 FORGE
*Valley Forge was the encampment site of the Continental Army during the winter of 1777-1778. 11,000 soldiers were stationed there, with hundreds dying of disease. The troops proved loyal to the cause of the revolution and to General George Washington.
*A reference to one of my ex-wives and I assume others' exes.

#98 CORNY
*"Schmaltzy" is a Yiddish word meaning "excessively sentimental".
*"Oy Vey" is a term borrowed from Yiddish, expressing dismay, exasperation or surprise, i.e. "Oh No!" or "Goodness gracious".

#99 MOULT
*Moult is the British spelling of Molt. It describes the casting off of an outer covering periodically. For example, the shedding of feathers, horns, shells, scales or hair or an outer layer.

See #315 LARVA for #99(2)

#101 SALAD
See #11 DWARF

#103 SPICY
See #58 BELLY

#106 FJORD

*Native Dancer (1950-1967), nicknamed the "Grey Ghost", was one of the most celebrated and accomplished thoroughbred race horses in American history. It was also the first horse made famous through the medium of television.

#109 GUILD

*In the middle ages European Jews were prohibited from joining artisan and merchant guilds. As they could not own land, what remained open to them was money lending, as portrayed by Shylock in Shakespeare's play *The Merchant of Venice*.

#110 ABACK

*In March of 2003, the U.S. invaded Iraq in what was referred to as a massive "shock and awe" bombing campaign that paved the way for American ground troops to converge on Baghdad.

*To talk smack is to make boastful or insulting remarks in order to demoralize or humiliate someone.

See #18 ABATE #45 CARGO

#111 MOTOR

*Gore-Tex is a company that specializes in waterproof outerwear

#113 HATCH

Flagrante delicto in Latin means in blazing offense. In other words in the very act of committing a crime or in the midst of sexual activity. A synonym is red-handed.

#114 HYPER

The Pied Piper of Hamelin is a tale originating from medieval folklore. The story inspired The Brothers Grimm legend, a Goethe verse and one of Robert Browning's best-known poems. The Piper was hired by Hamelin to rid the town of its plague of rats. Trailing after the hypnotic notes of the rat catcher's magical flute, the rodents politely file through the city gates to a river and subsequently, their doom. When the town refuses to pay the piper for his service he lures the town's children to the same doom.

#115 THUMB

*Tom Thumb is a character in English folklore. *The History of Tom Thumb* was published in 1621 and was the first fairy tale printed in English.

#119 DUTCH

*"Going Dutch" refers to dating in which each person pays their own expenses.

*A Nederlander is a Dutchman, citizen of or a person originating from the kingdom of the Netherlands (Holland).

#121 TWEED

*William Magear Tweed (1823-1878), widely known as Boss Tweed, was an American politician notable for being the political boss of Tammany Hall. This was the democratic party's political machine, which played a dominant role in the politics of New York City and the state in the 19th century.

#122 COMET

*Mark Twain's birth on November 30, 1835 came the same year that Halley's Comet approached near the earth at its perihelion. He died one day after the comet had once again reached its perihelion on April 21, 1910. The perihelion is the point nearest to the sun in the path of an orbiting celestial body.

See #290 NATAL

#125 STEED

*Sir Gawain, also known in many other forms and spellings, is a character in Arthurian legend, in which he is King Arthur's nephew and a Knight of the Round Table.

#128 FLING

See #164(2) BRING #285 LOWLY

#129 DOZEN

*The Dirty Dozen is a Robert Aldrich movie released in 1967. The plot is outlined in the limerick. One of the 12 convicts recruited to kill Nazis was played by Jim Brown (1936-2023), a former outstanding and popular fullback for the Cleveland Browns from 1957-1965.

#131 ERODE

*Entropy is a scientific concept in the world of physics that relates to the inherent capacity of matter that leads to a state of decay, deterioration, randomness and disorder. It is applied to the thermodynamics field, where it represents the lack of availability of a system's thermal energy for conversion into mechanical work, often interpreted as the degree of disorder or randomness in the system. The amount of entropy is a measure of the molecular disorder or randomness of a system.

#133 GOUGE

*The myth of Odysseus and the one eyed cyclops, Polyphemus, is one of the best known Greek myths, narrated by Homer in his *Odyssey*. This cyclops was one of the giant blacksmiths who had built Olympus for the gods.

#135 BRIAR
Uncle Remus Tales by Joel Chandler Harris was published in 1881. Remus is a fictional plantation slave who narrates a collection of African American folktales with moral lessons. The stories are written in Harris' interpretation of the dialect of African-American language in the deep South at the time. All the animal characters are referred to as 'Brer'. A Disney film: *Song of the South*, released in 1946, is based on Harris' book. Unfortunately, it is unlikely to be released in any format at this time, due to its sensitive theme regarding race. In the story referenced in the limerick, the rabbit comes across a "tar baby" who does not respond to his friendly greetings, infuriating the rabbit to such a degree that he gets himself covered with tar and is unable to move. At this point, the fox comes along and starts reveling in the rabbit's state, describing how he plans to eat him. The rabbit cleverly begs the fox to do whatever he pleases, as long as he doesn't throw him into the briar patch. The fox, easily goaded, does exactly this and the rabbit escapes.

#136 GREAT
*This is a perfect description of my wonderful wife.

See #163 PROVE (Einstein) #187(2) GRIPE (Regan). Freud and Churchill will have their limericks in subsequent volumes.

#141 DUCHY
See #289 SHAWL

#142 GROIN
Phenytoin (Dilantin) is a medication commonly used to control seizures. It works by slowing down the electrical impulses in the brain that cause the seizures.

#144 GROUP
See #339 ALBUM for #144(1)

#145 ROGUE
*In the summer of 1916, a rogue Great White shark attacked swimmers along the Jersey shore, triggering mass hysteria and launching the most extensive shark hunt in history. This event is well described in Michael Capuzzo's excellent book *Close To Shore*, published in 2001.

#147 SMART
*Rene Descartes (1596-1650) was a French philosopher, scientist and mathematician. His most important contribution was his insight into the connection between algebra and geometry. Descartes mistakenly thought the seat of the soul was in the pineal gland, which is triggered by darkness to secrete melatonin; light inhibits this process. In humans, this neuroendocrine organ is located in the midline of the brain outside the blood-brain barrier, and is attached to the roof of the third ventricle by a short stalk.

#148 PITHY
See #326 FARCE

#150 CHILL
The Barber of Seville or *The Useless Precaution* is an opera buffa in two acts composed by Gioachino Rossini (1792-1868) that premiered in 1816. It is based on a French comedy by the same name, written by Peirre Beaumarchais: (1732-1799).

#151 HERON
*Terrine originates from the French and refers to an earthenware dish in which foods are cooked and served. It is pronounced ter-ēn (tureen) which does not actually rhyme with heron (hər'-ən). Terrine should be intentionally mispronounced to rhyme with heron if reading aloud. The same is true of the second limerick in which "poulette", the French word for a young hen, is intentionally mispronounced to rhyme with egret by emphasizing the final "t" sound.

See #378 EGRET

#155 RADIO
*Tesla first filed the patent for radio in 1897 and it was granted to him in 1900. The Patent Office in the U.S. turned Marconi's application down in 1900 but reversed this decision in 1904, giving Marconi the patent for inventing radio. Marconi later won the Nobel Prize and Tesla sued for infringement. Marconi died in 1937. Tesla died in 1943. Six months after Tesla's death, the U.S. Supreme Court ruled that all of Marconi's patents were invalid and awarded the patents for radio to Tesla.

#156 ROUGE
*Rust is oxidized iron whose chemical formula is Fe_2O_3, also known as Ferric Oxide.

#158 RETCH
*A kvetch is a habitable complainer
*Hydrogen Sulfide (H_2S) is a gas that is responsible for the foul odor of flatulence. This compound is colorless, poisonous, corrosive and flammable, with trace amounts having the foul, pungent odor and taste of rotten eggs. It has significant adverse health effects with prolonged exposure or if high concentrations are inhaled. It is also known as sewer gas and swamp gas, and can be lethal to people who work in sewers and manure pits. If you wish to learn more on the fascinating and humorous subject of flatulence I recommend reading Mary Roach's book *Gulp: Adventures On the Alimentary Tract* (2013). Interestingly, women produce considerably more H_2S than men.

See #84(1) START

#159 WROTE
*"GOAT" is an acronym that means "Greatest Of All Time".
*The Oxford English Dictionary of Humorous quotations places Oscar Wilde (1854-1900) and George Bernard Shaw (1856-1950) in first and second place as most quoted. Jane Austen (1775-1817) is the most frequently quoted author on Goodreads while Shakespeare is the second.

See #30(2) PRIDE

#160 CLOCK
*In physics, spacetime is a mathematical model that combines the three dimensions of space and one dimension of time into a single four-dimensional manifold. Atomic clocks provide time that is extremely accurate, with an error of only one second in up to 100 million years (not spacetime).

See #93(2) GAMMA #179(1) TRACE

#161 TILDE
*A tilde (~) is a wavy line or graphene with several uses. When placed over a Spanish 'N', it changes the pronunciation to an NY sound. In mathematics, the symbol is used before a number to mean "about" or "approximately".
*A gimbal is a device that permits a body, such as a ship, to incline freely in any direction. It is a pivoted support that allows for an object's rotation about an axis.

#162 STORE
*Semper Fi is Latin for Always Faithful. Semper Fidelis is the motto of the United States Marines.
*Thor is a mythological demigod in Norse mythology who wields a hammer and is associated with lightning, thunder storms, and the protection of mankind. In modern times, he is a Marvel Entertainment super hero.

#163 PROVE
*Albert Einstein's formula ($E=mc^2$) states that the equivalent energy (E) can be calculated as the mass (m) multiplied by the speed of light (c= 3×10^8 m/s) squared. Mass-energy equivalence entails that the total mass of a system may change, but the total energy and momentum remain constant.

See #136(2) GREAT

#164 BRING
See #128 FLING #168 EXULT #236 PAUSE #285 LOWLY

#165 SOLVE

*Dame Agatha Mary Clarissa Christie (1890-1976) was an English writer known for her 66 detective novels and 14 short story collections, particularly those revolving around fictional detectives Hercule Poirot and Miss Marple. In 1926, she made international headlines by going missing for 11 days, following the breakdown of her marriage and the death of her mother.

#166 CHEAT

*Selling one's soul to the devil is a very popular theme in literature, theater and cinema. Plays and puppet theater based on this legend were popular throughout Germany in the 16th century. The story was popularized in England by Christopher Marlowe (1564-1593). Johann Wolfgang Goethe's (1749-1831) tragic play, *Faust*, concerning the same topic was first performed in 1829. To make a deal with the devil is a metaphor for collaboration with an evil regime and is referred to as a Faustian bargain.

*The movie was *Your Cheatin' Heart* (1964).

See #168 CHEAT #394(2) FLOCK for #166(1)

#168 EXULT

See #166(1) CHEAT #394(2) FLOCK

#169 USHER

*The first two limericks are based on Edgar Allan Poe's short stories: *The Fall of the House of Usher* and *The Cask of Amontillado*. (See also #317 STORY.)

*The Underground City of Montreal is an extensive underground network of shops, interconnected office towers, hotels, and residential and commercial complexes, including a metro. It is not the world's largest underground city; that distinction belongs to Elengubu (Derinkuyu) in Cappadocia, Turkey, which burrows more than 85 meters below the earth's surface. (See also #7 EVADE.)

See #7 EVADE #317(1) STORY #380(1) SEVER for #169(1)

#170 EPOCH

*The Holocene is the name given to the last 11,700 years of the Earth's history; the current epoch. It represents the time since the last major glacial epoch or ice age.

*Appomattox Court House in Virginia is the site where Confederate general Robert E. Lee surrendered his army to Union general Ulysses S. Grant on April 9, 1865, thus ending the Civil War.

#171 CHORD

*Carnegie Hall is a concert venue in Midtown Manhattan, New York City. Designed by American architect William Burnet Tuthill (1855-1929) and built by industrialist Andrew Carnegie (1835-1919), it is one of the most prestigious venues in the world for both classical and popular music.

#172 BREAK

*Charles Elwood Yeager (1923-2020) was a U.S. Air Force Brigadier General and test pilot who, in 1947, became the first pilot in history confirmed to have exceeded the speed of sound in level flight. The X-1 reached a speed of 700 miles-per-hour (Mach 1.06).

#173 RHINO

*RINO stands for "Republican In Name Only", a pejorative used to describe Republican politicians deemed insufficiently loyal to the party or misaligned with its ideology.

#176 MASSÉ

*In billiards, "massé" denotes a stroke made with an inclined cue which imparts a swerve to the ball.

*Jackie Gleason (1916-1987) played Minnesota Fats, the world title holder in professional pool, in the movie *The Hustler*, released in 1961. Paul Newman (1925-2008) played the upstart challenger, Fast Eddie.

#177 SONIC

*Ludwig van Beethoven (1770-1827) first noted a decline in hearing at age 28. By age 44 he was completely deaf. The cause was either overgrowth of bone resulting in compression of his eighth cranial nerves (due to Paget's disease) or lead intoxication.

*When one hears a sonic boom, that is not the sound of the "sound barrier" being broken. That sound is made continuously by any object that is passing through the air faster than sound can.

#178 VITAL

*A Gorgon is a creature in Greek mythology. The term most commonly refers to three sisters who have hair made of living venomous snakes and horrifying visages that turn those that behold them to stone. Medusa is the best known of the three.

#179 TRACE

*In subatomic physics, every type of particle is associated with an antiparticle with the same mass but opposite physical (electric) charge. For example, the antiparticle of the negatively charged electron is the positively charged positron. Particle-antiparticle pairs can annihilate each other, thereby producing photons.

See #93(2) GAMMA #160(1) CLOCK

#180 USING

*Aspirin irreversibly inhibits the enzyme cyclo-oxygenase (COX-1) which is needed to reduce thromboxane in platelets. This makes them less sticky and less effective in activating platelets to aggregate, which leads to increased risk of bleeding and bruising.

See #74 BLEED

#182 CHAMP

*Casius Clay made his professional boxing debut on October 29, 1960, after winning the gold medal at the 1960 Olympics. After that he proceeded to win his first 19 fights, with 15 wins by knockout. On February 25, 1964, 22 year old Cassius Clay dethroned Sonny Liston to become heavyweight boxing champion. He won the world heavyweight championship on three separate occasions. On March 6, 1964, Clay shocked the boxing establishment by announcing he had accepted the teachings of the Nation of Islam and changed his name to Muhammad Ali.

*On the Waterfront is a 1954 American crime drama film, directed by Elia Kazan (1909-2003), starring Marlon Brando (1924-2004) and Eva Marie Saint (b. 1924), who won the Academy Award for Best Supporting Actress for her performance. At 100 years old, she is the oldest living Academy Award winner. The film won a total of 8 Academy Awards including: Best Picture, Best Actor (Brando), Best Director (Kazan). Brando's award statue was stolen.

#186 CRAZE

*In Greek mythology, Terpsichore is one of the nine Muses and goddess of dance and chorus. "Terpsichorean" refers to anything relating to dance. The nine muses are daughters of Zeus and Mnemosyne (memory personified) and personifications of knowledge and the arts, especially poetry, dance, literature and music.

#187 GRIPE

*President Ronald Reagan's first big screen role as an actor was playing ill-fated football star George Gipp in the 1940 film, Knute Rockne All-American. In a famous scene, the dying, bed-ridden Gipp (nicknamed the Gipper), urges his college teammates to win a critical football game in his honor. That role catapulted Reagan to fame, and the nickname "the Gipper" stuck.

See #136(2) GREAT for #187(2)

#190 ACUTE

*Pythagoras of Samos (570-495 BC) was an ancient Ionian Greek philosopher, polymath and mathematician. He is credited with many mathematical and scientific discoveries, including the Pythagorean theorem of triangles ($a^2+b^2=c^2$), the sphericity of the Earth, the identity of the morning and evening stars as the planet Venus, and others.

#191 FERRY

*Charon, the ferryman of Hades, carries the souls of the dead across the river Styx, a body of water that separates the worlds of the living and the dead. The obol is a coin placed under the tongue of the deceased to pay the fare to cross the river. One obol represents in weight one half of a scruple of silver or one sixth of a drachma.

#192 ASIDE

The Strange Case of Dr Jekyll and Mr Hyde is an 1886 novella by Scottish author Robert Louis Stevenson (1850-1894). It is one of the most famous pieces of English literature and a defining book of the gothic horror genre.

#194 TROLL

See #219(1) KNOLL for #194(1)

#195 UNIFY

*The transcontinental railroad, commonly known as the iron horse, was a network of railroads that connected the East and West Coasts of the United States in the late 1800s. To complete the transcontinental railroad, the Union Pacific and Central Pacific rails met in Promontory Summit, Utah on May 10, 1869. A golden spike was driven into the ground upon completion. 1800 miles of track were laid to connect the East and West coasts.

#196 REBUS

*A rebus is a puzzle in which words are represented by combinations of letters and pictures.

*Occam's razor is a principle attributed to 14th century friar William of Ockham (1287-1347). It states that if you have two competing ideas to explain the same phenomenon, choose the simpler one. It is also referred to as the law of parsimony.

#198 TRUSS

*Hyperthermia is an abnormally high body temperature. Inducing hyperthermia to treat cancer is an infrequently used treatment which originated with surgical oncologist William B. Cooly (1862-1936). In 1891, Cooly used a mixture of bacterial toxins (Cooly's toxin) to induce hyperthermia. This treatment represented a precursor to modern immunotherapy.

See #259(1) BRINE for #198(2)

#199 SIEGE

*The Battle of Vienna in 1683 took place after the imperial city had been besieged by the Ottoman Empire for two months. The siege ended after a baker heard the Turks tunneling under the walls of the city and alerted the military. The tunnel was collapsed on the Turks, thus eliminating the threat and saving the city. The baker baked a crescent shaped pastry in the shape of the Turkish flag's Islamic emblem, the crescent moon, so that when his fellow Austrians bit into the croissant, they would be symbolically devouring the Turks.

#200 TIGER

*The Lady, or the Tiger? is a short story written by Frank R. Stockton in 1882, for publication in the magazine *The Century*. This story has become an allegorical expression or signifier for a problem that is unsolvable.

*William Blake (1757-1827) was an English poet, painter and printmaker. Largely unrecognized in his lifetime, he is now considered a seminal figure in the history of poetry and visual art of the Romantic Age. He is primarily known for his poem "The Tyger" published in 1789 in the book *Songs of Innocence and Experience*.

#201 BANAL

*Pyrokinesis is the purported psychic ability that allows an individual to create and control fire with the mind.

See #66 PANEL

#202 SLUMP

*Quasimodo is the fictional character and the main protagonist of the novel *The Hunchback of Notre Dame* by Victor Hugo (1802-1885), published in 1831. He was born with a hunchback deformity and is the bell ringer of Notre Dame Cathedral.

#203 CRANK

*Max Karl Ernst Planck (1858-1947) was a German theoretical physicist who discovered energy quanta (particles) for which he won the Nobel Prize in 1918.

#205 QUERY

*"Action at a distance" is the concept in physics that an object can be affected without being physically touched by another object. As an example, gravitational forces are action at a distance forces that act between two objects even when they are held some distance apart.

*Concomitance is the occurrence or existence together or in connection with one another. In theology, concomitance is the fact of existing or occurring together with something else. It is a theological doctrine that the body and blood of Christ are each present in both the bread and the wine of the Eucharist.

#206 DRINK

*Ximena is a fairly common female name in Chile.

*Verbena, also known as vervain or verveine, is a genus in the family Verbenaceae which contains 150 species of annual and perennial herbaceous flowering plants. The leaf has a pleasant lemony scent and slightly minty taste. It makes delicious tea.

*The ocarina is a wind musical instrument that is a type of vessel flute. A typical ocarina is an enclosed space with 4 to 12 finger holes and a mouthpiece that projects from the body. It is an ancient Central American instrument that has been crafted and played for more than 4500 years.

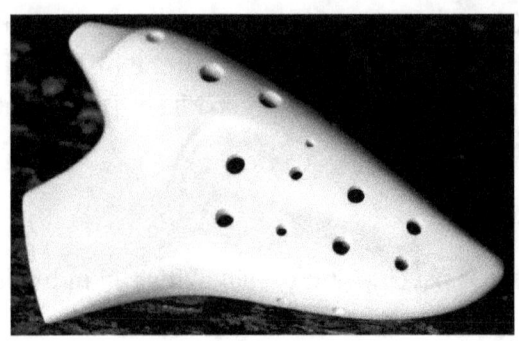

Picture credit: fityclub.

#207 FAVOR

*Rodney George Laver (b. 1938) is an Australian tennis player who won four major singles championships in one year (1962) and was the first to repeat this grand slam (1969). He is considered one of the greatest players in the history of tennis.

#210 PANIC

*In ancient Greek religion and mythology, Pan is the god of the wild, shepherds and flocks, and rustic music, as well as a companion of the nymphs. He is a satyr. His mother was a nature sprite or nymph.

#212 SHIRE

*Lord of the Rings is an epic fantasy novel by English scholar John Ronald Reuel Tolkien (1892-1973), published in three parts in 1954. The story began as a sequel to Tolkien's 1937 children's book *The Hobbit*, but eventually developed into a much larger work. It is one of the best-selling book series ever written. Award winning adaptations have been made for radio, theater and film.

#215 ROBOT

*The Three Laws of Robotics are a set of rules devised by science fiction author Issac Azimov (1920-1992) in his 1942 short story *Runaround*. The Three Laws are:

1: A robot may not injure or allow harm to come to a human being.
2: A robot must obey orders by a human being unless such orders conflict with the first law.
3: A robot must protect its own existence as long as such protection does not conflict with the First or Second Law.

*Incidentally, Azimov has published, with John Ciardi, a substantial number of bawdry limericks.

*Forbidden Planet is a sci-fi classic released in 1956 starring Walter Pidgeon, Leslie Nielson and Anne Francis. I have pleasant memories of watching this film with classmates many times just before final exams at MIT, cheering and booing to let off steam.

#216 PRICK

*"Schtick" is a Yiddish word: gimmick associated with a particular person.

See #51 LINEN

#217 WINCE

*A blintz is a traditional Jewish cuisine that consists of a thin pancake, similar to a crepe, that is usually filled with a creamy cheese mixture and pan fried to give it a crispy outside. The plural of blintz is blintzes.

#219 KNOLL

*In conspiracy theories of the death of President John Fitzgerald Kennedy (1917-1963), it is suggested that the real assassin was an unidentified gunman on a grassy knoll, overlooking the route of his motorcade in Dallas. Lee Harvey Oswald (1939-1963) is considered to be the person responsible.

See #194(1) TROLL for #219(2)

#221 WHACK

*Blaise Pascal (1623-1662) was a French mathematician, physicist, inventor, philosopher and Catholic writer. He was a child prodigy whose earliest mathematical work was on conic sections (See Limerick #175). Among his achievements were: probability theory, the invention of one of the first mechanical calculators, making important contributions to the study of fluids, and clarification of the concepts of pressure and vacuum.

#222 MOUNT

*Pompeii is a vast archeological site in Southern Italy, near the coast of the bay of Naples. Once a thriving and sophisticated Roman city, Pompeii was buried under ash and pumice after the catastrophic eruption of Mount Vesuvius in 79 A.D.

*Edmund Hillary (1919-2008) and sherpa Tenzing Norgay (1914-1986) became the first explorers to reach the summit of Mount Everest (29,035 feet above sea level, the highest point on earth) on May 29, 1953.

#226 LIGHT

*A photon is a tiny particle that comprises waves of electromagnetic radiation. As shown by Maxwell, photons are just electric fields traveling through space. They have no charge, no resting mass, and travel at the speed of light.

#232 SKILL

*A blue whale can eat up to four tons of krill daily; it is the vast majority of their diet. They lunge through large swarms of krill with their mouth open, taking in more food in one mouthful than any other animal on earth.

#233 ELDER

*An Old Testament patriarch, Methuselah's life span was recorded at 969 years; he is considered the longest living human. The most logical explanation for his longevity is due to a mistranslation of 969 lunar months as years which would make his actual age in a range of 78 to 97 years. Literalists have other explanations. Methuselah's wife was Edna. I could not find any information on her life span.

#235 HUMOR

*Anyone who grew up in New York City during the 1950s will understand this memory. The "Good Humor Man" was the driver of the ice-cream truck.

*A Pseudotumor or false tumor is an enlargement that resembles a tumor. It may result from inflammation, accumulation of fluid, or other causes. It may or may not regress spontaneously.

#236 PAUSE

See #164 BRING

#237 ULCER

*Heliobacter Pylori is a motile spiral bacterium. It can damage the stomach lining, cause gastritis and peptic ulcers, and is associated with gastric cancer and lymphoma. This association was not discovered until 1982 when two Australians, Professor Barry Marshall and Doctor Robin Warren, reported the association for which they were awarded the Nobel Prize in Physiology and Medicine in 2005.

#239 ROBIN

*There are a number of legends regarding the robin and Jesus. One states that the robin's breast is red because of his association with Christ's crucifixion. When Jesus was on the road to Calvary it is said that a robin plucked a thorn from Christ's temple and a drop of his blood fell on the robin's breast turning it red.

See #248(1) THORN #260 CLOTH

#240 CYNIC

*Cynicism was a School of Philosophy founded in Athens by Antisthenes (455-366 BC), a student of Socrates. The school lasted 800 years after Diogenes, its best known disciple, and was a major influence on Stoicism. Diogenes actually did live in a ceramic jar.

#241 AROMA

*MOMA is an abbreviation for The Museum of Modern Art in New York City.

*The Shona people are part of the Bantu ethnic group, native to Southern Africa. Primarily, they live in Zimbabwe where they form the majority of the population.

#243 SHAKE

*"Shake, Rattle and Roll" is a song written by Jessie Stone. The original was recorded by Big Joe Turner, and it is ranked number 127 on the Rolling Stone magazine's list of the 500 Greatest Songs of All Time. "Shake, Rattle and Roll" is also the title of an early rock and roll compilation album by Decca Records in 1955, featuring music by Bill Haley & His Comets.

*Parkinson's Disease is a group of neurological disorders characterized by hypokinesia, tremors, and muscular rigidity. It is caused by a decrease in production of dopamine in a portion of the brain called the substantia nigra. This disease is also referred to as the Shaking Palsy or Paralysis Agitans and was first described by James Parkinson (1755-1824), an English surgeon, apothecary, geologist and paleontologist.

#244 DODGE

*Madam Theresa Lafarge is a fictional character and main antagonist of the 1859 novel *A Tale of Two Cities* by Charles Dickens (1812-1879). She is a tireless worker for the French Revolution, memorably knitting beside the guillotine during executions.

#247 OTHER

*Holograph is an image produced by holography. Also called a hologram.
*Homograft is a graft of tissue taken from a donor of the same species as the recipient.

See #307 PLANT #359(1+2) DONOR #390(1) LIVER for #247(1)

#248 THORN

See #239 ROBIN #260 CLOTH for #248(1)

#249 TROVE

*By Jove is an idiom that expresses surprise or emphasis. By Jove entered our language in the late 14th century as a way to refer to Jupiter, the Roman god (whom the Greeks called Zeus). It is a euphemism for "by Jesus" or "by God".

#251 VIVID

See #298(2) CHUNK #387(1) MADAM for #251(1)

#253 CHANT

*Gregorian chant is the central tradition of Western plainchant, a form of monophonic, unaccompanied sacred song in Latin of the Roman Catholic Church. It developed mainly in western and central Europe during the 9th and 10th centuries.

See #384(2) VOICE

#254 CHOKE

*Debbie Does Dallas is a 1978 pornographic film, starring Bambi Woods.

#256 NASTY

*The MET refers to the Metropolitan Opera House in New York City. It opened in 1966, replacing the original 1883 Metropolitan Opera House.

*The Hitler regime passed a forced sterilization law in 1933. It targeted neuropsychiatric patients with conditions such as feeblemindedness, schizophrenia, and epilepsy, as well as many other conditions. In the 12 years of the nazi regime, 400,000 people were forcibly sterilized.

#257 MOURN

*Mozart's *Requiem in D minor, K. 626* is a requiem mass by Wolfgang Amadeus Mozart (1756-1791). He composed part of the requiem in Vienna in late 1791, but though he worked on it up until his death on December 5th of that same year, it remained unfinished. Franz Xaver Süssmayer composed a completed version of the requiem in 1972, at the request and commission of Count Franz von Walsegg. A partial performance of the requiem was played at Mozart's funeral.

*"Shiva" means "seven", signifying the seven days of mourning in the Jewish faith. "Sitting Shiva" is a time to gain spiritual and emotional healing by joining together to mourn the death of a family member.

See #83 LAPEL for #257(2)

#259 BRINE

*The oldest intact shipwreck is the 2400 year old Greek ship *The Odysseus*. It has been carbon dated to 400 BC. The wreck was discovered in 2017, located 1.3 miles under the surface of the Black Sea. Many shipwrecks found in the Black Sea are almost perfectly preserved due to the lack of oxygen in the sea's dead zone.

*"Davy Jones locker" is a metaphor for the oceanic abyss. It is a euphemism for drowning or shipwrecks in which sailors and ships remain consigned to the depths of the ocean. The origins of the name "Davy Jones" or "the sailor's devil" are unclear.

See #198 TRUSS for #259(1)

#260 CLOTH

*The Shroud of Turin (The Holy Shroud) is a length of linen cloth bearing the negative image of a man. Some believe the image depicts Jesus and that the fabric is the burial shroud he was wrapped in after crucifixion. In 1988, radiocarbon dating established that the shroud was from the Middle ages (1260-1390), but this is controversial as the dating of a fragment of the cloth from its edge may have been done on repaired material after a 1532 fire which nearly burned the cloth. DNA testing demonstrated residual human DNA. The blood type was AB. Only 3.2% of the population have AB blood type. It is 600% more common among Jews in Northern Palestine. The shroud continues to be studied and remains a controversial issue among scientists and biblical scholars. For further details, see *Holy Evidence* by Luca Cacciatore and Kimberly Carberry (Newsmax, April 2023).

See #239 ROBIN #248(1) THORN

#261 HOARD
*"Ordure" means "excrement" or something that is morally degrading.

#262 SWEET
*"Sweet Caroline" was first played at Fenway Park in 1997 by an employee in charge of music at the park. It was played as a tribute to a friend who had given birth to a baby named Caroline. The song caught on and has played before the bottom of the eighth inning since.

#263 MONTH
*The rhyme is as follows: "30 days hath September, April, June and November. All the rest have 31, excepting February alone, and that has 28 days clear and 29 in each leap year."

#265 WATCH
*Paul Revere's Ride was a poem by Henry Wadsworth Longfellow (1807-1882), written in 1860. It commemorates the American patriot Paul Revere (1735-1818) who rode to alert the Continental army of the manner of the British arrival on April 18, 1775.

#267 FOCUS
*As we age there is a gradual loss of one's eye's ability to focus on nearby objects. This is known as presbyopia, and it usually becomes noticeable in our mid 40's. This leads one to read more comfortably at increasing distance from our eye, eventually forcing us to read at arm's length. Thus, our arms eventually get too short and reading glasses become mandatory.
*Atherosclerosis is build-up of fats, cholesterol, and other substances in the artery walls (plaque). This is associated with aging.

#268 SMELT
*Hephaestus is the Greek god of fire, volcanoes, blacksmithing and metalworking.

#269 TEASE
*ACME was the company best known for providing instruments of destruction to any character within the Looney Tunes universe; most notably Wily Coyote.

#271 MOVIE
*A doobie is slang for a marijuana cigarette or joint.

See #54(2) BOOBY for #271(1)

#272 SAUTE
See #284 STOVE

#273 ALLOW
*The first vaccine against poliomyelitis was released in 1955 by Jonas Salk (1914-1995). This was an inactivated vaccine, given intramuscularly. A live attenuated oral vaccine developed by Albert Bruce Sabin (1906-1993) became available in 1960. It has not been used in the United States since 2000.

#274 RENEW
*During REM (Rapid Eye Movement) sleep, your eyes move around rapidly, but do not send any visual signal to the brain. NREM (Non Rapid Eye Movement) sleep is important in memory consolidation. REM sleep is associated with dreaming. NREM sleep constitutes 75 to 80% of total sleep time while REM sleep constitutes the remaining 20 to 25% of sleep time.

#277 PURGE
See #93(1) GAMMA for #277(1)

#278 CHEST
*MI or myocardial infarction is medical jargon for a heart attack.

#279 DEPOT
*Dengue fever is a mosquito-borne illness that occurs in tropical and subtropical regions of the world. Mild dengue fever causes a high fever and flu-like symptoms while the severe form of the disease (dengue hemorrhagic fever) can cause serious bleeding, shock and death. The cause is a Flavivirus transmitted by the bite of infected Aedes mosquitos.

See #399 MIDGE for #279(2)

#281 NYMPH
*The Nereids in Greek mythology are sea nymphs, the 50 daughters of the "Old Man of the Sea", Nereus. They often accompany Poseidon, the god of the sea, and can be friendly and helpful to sailors. They appear fully human and famously beautiful, but unlike a mermaid they do not develop scales or tails upon contact with water.
*Sirens have bird bodies with a tail and have human heads. Sirens are dangerous and lure mariners to destruction with their seductive singing.
*In certain circles that believe in the fae (fairies) and the ways that they used to interact with our world, there is a claim that they were chased away by humanity and the introduction of technology. As a result, they have escaped to a different plane and bide their time until they can return home, interacting with the world in minor ways from beyond.

#282 FOUND
*Both limericks are based on the author's life experiences.

#284 STOVE
See #272 SAUTE

#285 LOWLY
See #128 FLING #164(2) BRING

#286 SNOUT
**Cyrano de Bergerac* is a play written in 1897 by Edmund Rostand (1868-1918). The entire play is written in verse. Cyrano is a nobleman and soldier serving in the French army in 1640. He has many talents including being an excellent duelist, a gifted poet and a musical artist, however, his obnoxiously large nose causes him to doubt himself and prevents him from expressing his love for his beautiful cousin Roxane.

*Durante (1893-1980) always finished his television shows with "Goodnight Mrs Calabash wherever you are". This was a tribute to his first wife Jeanne Olsen (and their inside joke) who died in 1943.

#287 TROPE
*A trope is a word or expression used in a figurative sense; figure of speech. A common or overused theme: cliché.

#288 FEWER
*A less than sign is represented as <. Greater than is >. There is no fewer than sign.

#289 SHAWL
*Pashmina is a fine wool similar to cashmere, made from the undercoat of domestic Himalayan goats.

See #141(2) DUCHY #169(2) USHER

#290 NATAL
Mark Twain was the pen name of Samuel Clemens. He was born shortly after Halley's Comet appeared in 1835. He died of a heart attack one day after it reached its perihelion (when it appeared brightest) in 1910. One year before his death, Clemens predicted his death coinciding with the comet's reappearance.

See #0 CIGAR #122 COMET

#292 FORAY

*Flyting is an exchange of insults in verse form. This contest of verbal abuse was remarkable for its fierceness and extravagance. By the 9th century it became a full-fledged cultural cornerstone among the Norse and the Saxons.

#294 STAIR

*The second limerick is not an original, but one I admire and could never improve upon.

#295 BLACK

*Angela Yvonne Davis (b. 1944) is an American Marxist, feminist political activist and professor at the University of California, Santa Cruz. In 1970, as a member of the Black Panthers, she was on the FBI's most wanted list for her involvement in the killing of several people. This was during an attempted court room escape at the trial of George Jackson, who was on trial for killing a prison guard. The guns used were registered to her. She served 18 months in jail. Ironically, recent DNA evidence has revealed she has ancestral roots to the Mayflower.

*This limerick was written by my goofy granddaughter, whose last name happens to be Black. She has been indispensable in the reediting of the limericks in Volume 1. She is responsible for many of the 6th lines in this volume.

#296 SQUAD

*The Mossad is the national intelligence agency of Israel. It is one of the main branches of the Israeli intelligence community, which also includes Aman (military intelligence) and Shin Bet (internal security).

#298 CHUNK

*To spelunk is to explore natural caves. Geologists do a lot of spelunking.

See #251(1) VIVID #387(1) MADAM for #298(2)

#300 SHAME

*Antoine Dominique Domino Jr., known as Fats Domino (1928-2017), was an American singer and songwriter. One of the pioneers of rock and roll music, he sold more than 65 million records, the most popular of which were "Ain't That A Shame" and "Blueberry Hill".

#302 AMPLE

*The hippocampus is the part of the brain that is integral to the limbic system. It plays an essential part in regulating learning, memory encoding, consolidation, as well as spatial navigation.

*Paresthesia refers to the sensation known as "pins and needles" after having an extremity "fall asleep". Formication or a sensation of insects crawling on the skin is a less common form of paresthesia. Paresthesia can result from stroke, multiple sclerosis, transverse myelitis, encephalitis, and many other disorders.

#307 PLANT
See # 247(1) OTHER #359(1+2) DONOR #390(1) LIVER

#308 OLIVE
*Giacomo Puccini (1858-1924) was an Italian opera composer. He is regarded as the most successful proponent of Italian Opera after Verdi. His most renowned works are *La Bohème* (1896), *Tosca* (1900), *Madame Butterfly* (1904) and *Turandot* (1924), which are among the most frequently performed and recorded of all operas.

#309 INERT
*An opossum did indeed fool me as when I came upon it it looked quite dead. I prodded it and did everything but take its pulse which fooled me into believing it was indeed dead despite the fact that I am a competent diagnostician in the practice of medicine. When I returned 5 minutes later to dispose of it, the rascal was not there. Fortunately for my reputation as a physician, no witnesses were present.
*A noble gas is any of seven chemical elements that make up Group VIII of the periodic table. They are Helium (He), Neon (Ne), Argon (Ar), Krypton (Kr), Xenon (Xe), Radon (Rn), and Oganesson (Og) with an atomic number of 118. They have long been believed to be totally unreactive, but compounds of xenon, krypton, and radon are now known. They are chemically unreactive because the atoms of noble gases already have complete outer electron shells.

#311 HEIST
*William Frances Sutton (1901-1980) was an American bank robber. During his 40 year robbery career, he stole an estimated 2 million dollars. He spent more than half of his adult life in prison and escaped three times. When asked why he robbed banks, his response was "because that's where the money is". This is the origin of Sutton's law which when applied to medicine is: focus on the obvious rather than trying to diagnose relatively uncommon medical disorders.

#313 ZESTY
*This is the first Wordle word that I undertook.

#315 LARVA
See #99 MOULT

#317 STORY
The Emperor's New Clothes is a literary folktale written by Danish author Hans Christian Anderson (1805-1875). It is about a vain emperor who gets exposed (literally) before his subjects. The tale has been translated into over 100 languages.

See #169(1) USHER #380(1) SEVER

#318 HAIRY

*Hairy tongue is an abnormal coating on the dorsal (upper) surface of the tongue. It is a common, temporary and harmless condition which occurs in 13% of the population. It results from the defective shedding of the tongue's covering tissue, with a buildup of keratin which elongates the filiform papillae (taste buds).

#320 HOMER

*Casey at the Bat: A Ballad of the Republic, Sung in the Year 1888 is a mock-heroic poem written in 1888 by Ernest Thayer. It features a dramatic narrative about a baseball game. It was later popularized by DeWolf Hopper in many vaudeville performances. It has become one of the best known poems in American literature.

See #359(2) DONOR

#321 BADGE

*Stephan Crane (1871-1900) was an American poet, novelist and short storywriter. Prolific throughout his short life, he wrote notable works in the Realist tradition. He is recognized by modern critics as one of the most innovative writers of his generation

*A hajj is one of the 5 pillars of Islam central to muslim belief. Hajj is the pilgrimage to Mecca that every Muslim must take at least once in their lifetime if they are able. Hajj can also be spelled hagjdj or hadj.

#323 CANNY

*Amedeo Clemente Modigliani (1884-1920) was an Italian painter and sculptor who worked mainly in France. He is known for his portraits and nudes in a modern style: characterized by a surreal elongation of faces, necks and figures that were not well received during his lifetime.

#325 GECKO

*The Ekeko is a traditional god of luck and prosperity in the occidental territory of Bolivia.

*Domenikos Theotokópoulos (1541-1614), most widely known as El Greco, was a Greek painter, sculptor and architect of the Spanish Renaissance. El Greco was his nickname. His dramatic and expressionistic style was met with puzzlement by his contemporaries but found appreciation in the 20th century. He is regarded as a precursor of both Expressionism and Cubism.

*Geckos are small, carnivorous lizards that are found on every continent except Antarctica. Geckos use sounds to warn off any approaching animal, to show aggression or dominance, to attract mates and when they are feeling threatened. It is written that they emit a series of chirping or chapping sounds. However, I am currently in the jungle of Northern Thailand near the Golden Triangle and have heard the gecko sound for the first time. To me it sounds like a loud "geck oh" that is emitted sharply, loud and clear. That is what inspired this limerick, which was not in the first publication of Wordle Limericks Volume 1.

#326 FARCE
See #148 PITHY

#329 METAL
*A coven is an assembly of witches.

#331 DELVE
*"The Twelve Days of Christmas" is an English Christmas Carol published in 1780. It is a classic example of a cumulative song. The lyrics detail a series of increasingly numerous gifts given on each of the twelve days of Christmas.

#332 BEING
*When the term "being" came into use in the 14th century, the church had decreed that God and angels were self-aware "beings" of the highest order. Genesis stated that humans had been made in the image of God, so they were accorded the title of being.

#334 GLASS
*Phillip Glass (b. 1937) is an American composer and pianist, regarded as one of the most influential composers of the late 20th century. His works have been associated with minimalism, built up from repetitive phrases and shifting layers.
*Silica is Silicon Dioxide (SiO_2), limestone is Calcium Carbonate ($CaCO_3$), soda ash is Sodium Carbonate ($NaCO_3$).

#335 GAMER
*A study conducted by the University of Montreal on individuals between the ages of 55 and 75 found that playing video games lead to an increase in gray matter in the hippocampus. Loss of gray matter is associated with Alzheimer's and other forms of dementia.

#339 ALBUM
See #144(1) GROUP

#342 TIARA
*Leptospira is a spiral shaped spirochete bacterium which causes Leptospirosis (also referred to as Weil's Disease). Humans can acquire this disease through contact with urine of infected animals.

#343 CREPT
*Giacomo Girolamo Casanova (1725-1798) was an Italian adventurer and author. His autobiography: *Histoire de ma vie* (Story of My Life), is regarded as one of the most authentic and provocative sources of information about the customs of European social life during the 18th century. He became famous for his complicated and elaborate affairs with women.

#344 BAYOU

*Cajuns are descendants of French settlers who moved to an area of Canada known as Acadia in modern day Nova Scotia. After Acadia became a British colony in 1710, many people of French ancestry left rather than pledge allegiance to the British crown. The majority settled in Louisiana. English speakers shortened the name of Acadians to 'Cadians and eventually to Cajuns. These new arrivals to the Louisiana territory were isolated and spoke French. To work they had to learn English. Cajun English today is mostly American English with French words and accent.

*In present day Louisiana, Creole generally refers to people of mixed colonial French, African-American and Native American ancestry.

#345 ATOLL

*Robinson Crusoe is a novel by Daniel Defoe (1660-1731), published in 1719. The book is presented as an autobiography of the title character, a castaway who spends 28 years on a remote tropical desert island near the coast of Venezuela, encountering cannibals, captives and mutineers before being rescued.

#346 MANOR

*The four limericks tell the story of Tarzan of the Apes as written by Edgar Rice Burroughs (1875-1950). Tarzan is a series of 24 adventure novels published between 1912 and 1966. It has been adapted many times for radio, television, stage and cinema. My version is based on the 1984 movie Greystoke. The first and fourth limericks contain the word manor. The second and third break my rules as they do not contain the word manor. They are used as a vehicle to tell the story and connect the first and fourth limericks.

#350 FROTH

*Porphyria is a group of genetic metabolic disorders caused by a deficiency of one or more of the enzymes required to produce a porphyrin ring structure, which is an essential component of the hemoglobin molecule that iron attaches to.

*Proteinuria (also albuminuria) signifies the presence of protein in the urine. This indicates a disturbance in the kidney filter, the glomerulus. There are many causes, including hypertension and diabetes, as well as benign conditions. Symptoms include foamy urine and swelling.

*Beer is thought to have been invented by the Sumerians, who lived in what is now Iraq, around 8000 BC. Ancient tablets have revealed the original brewers were women.

#351 DEPTH

*The Mariana Trench is an oceanic trench located in the western Pacific Ocean, 200 kilometers east of the Mariana Islands. This deepest known point of the seabed of earth is called the Challenger Deep. It is 35,876 feet deep and is located at the southern end of the Mariana Trench. Mount Everest, the highest point on earth is 28,035 feet tall.

#352 GLOOM

*In December of 1952, a severe air pollution event affected London. It was referred to as the Great Smog of London. Unusually cold weather, combined with an anticyclone and windless conditions, collected airborne particles arising from coal burning and formed a thick layer of smog over the city, which lasted five days. More than 4,000 people died due to related health issues.

#353 FLOOD

*Hurricane Katrina was a devastating Category 5 Atlantic hurricane that caused 1,392 fatalities and between $100 billion to $150 billion in damage, primarily in New Orleans in August of 2005.

#354 TRAIT

*Both arose and arouse have one sense of "waking up", but usually "arouse" has a sexual connotation, whilst "arise" simply means to wake up or stand up. Example: I arose early with the intent to arouse my still sleeping wife for an early morning screw.

#355 GIRTH

*The equatorial girth of the earth or its circumference is 24,901.461 miles.

See #386 BERTH

#357 GOOSE

*The Spruce Goose was first conceived during World War II. It was intended to circumvent the sinking of ships by German submarines by using a huge plane to transport troops to Europe. Howard Hughes (1905-1976) designed and built it. Despite its name, the aircraft was made entirely of birch wood, due to restrictions on the use of steel and aluminum, and was six times larger than any aircraft of that era. It flew only one time in 1947, in Long Beach, California.

See #358(1) FLOAT

#358 FLOAT

*Archimedes of Syracuse (287-212 BC) was a Greek mathematician, physicist, engineer and inventor. He is regarded as one of the leading scientists of antiquity. He did the first calculation of pi and is best known for the Archimedes Principle of buoyancy, which states that a body immersed in a fluid is subjected to an upwards force equal to the weight of the displaced fluid.

See #357(1) GOOSE for #358(1)

#359 DONOR

*Agoraphobia is an anxiety disorder characterized by fear of places and situations that might cause panic, helplessness, or embarrassment.

*Hippocrates of Cos (450-380 B.C.) was a physician who is considered the father of modern medicine. In his 70+ books he described, in a scientific manner, many diseases and their treatment after detailed observation. He devised the Hippocratic Oath, a code of ethics for physicians which all physicians swear to observe to this day.

See #247(1) OTHER #307 PLANT #390(1) LIVER for #359(2)

#360 ATONE

*Alphonse Gabriel Capone (1899-1947), a.k.a. "Scarface", was an American gangster who attained notoriety during prohibition. His seven year reign as a crime boss ended when he went to prison at age 33, for 11 years. While he was in prison he developed signs of neurosyphilis.

*Neurosyphilis is an infection of the central nervous system in a patient within the late or tertiary phase of the infection. Symptoms include: headache, confusion, seizures, cranial nerve deficits, and others.

*Circumcised men have a lower risk of syphilis infection and other sexually transmitted diseases (STDs) than uncircumcised men.

#361 PRIMO

*Quoted from a UCLA psych paper, emo is a subculture that originated from a melodic subgenre of punk rock music, also known as "emotional hardcore". It has evolved to become a well-recognised slang term to describe a group with particular preferences in clothes, music, and behaviors.

#364 CACAO

*Cacao is the raw unprocessed version of cocoa. If you happen to be in Sedona, Arizona and love chocolate in all of its raw and delicious power, drop into my daughter's shop: "Living Chocolate".

#366 INPUT

*The occipital lobes sit in the back of the brain and operates the visual processing area of the brain. It is responsible for visuospatial processing, distance and depth perception, color determination, object and face recognition, and memory formation.

#368 AWFUL

*Nematodes are elongated cylindrical worms that are frequently parasitic in plants and animals, or free living in soil or water. Examples of parasitism in humans include: ascaris, hookworms, pinworms and whipworms.

#369 BRINK

*The Cuban Missile Crisis of October, 1962 was a 35 day confrontation between the United States and the Soviet Union. Russia secretly deployed nuclear missiles in Cuba. President Kennedy blockaded Russian ships from reaching Cuba. The crisis was ultimately resolved. Russia withdrew the missiles after the United States agreed to withdraw nuclear missiles from Turkey and Italy and agreed not to invade Cuba.

See #21(1) DEATH #382 FLUFF for #369(2)

#370 SMITE

*In *The Old Testament*, the book of Exodus accounts the events leading up to the liberation of the Jewish people from slavery in Egypt, including Moses' pleading with the Pharaoh to free his people. When he refuses, God sends a series of 10 plagues to pressure the Egyptian ruler. Only the 10th results in Pharaoh's relinquishment. (The plagues are detailed in the footnote for 657 LOCUS in Volume 2, to be published.)

#378 EGRET

*An operon is a genetic regulatory system found in bacteria and their viruses in which genes coding for functionally related proteins are clustered along the DNA.

See #151 HERON

#380 SEVER

*Edgar Allan Poe (1809-1849) published the poem "Annabel Lee" in 1849. It was his last complete poem. Like many of his poems it explores the theme of the death of a beautiful woman. The love between the narrator and the dead beauty is so strong that even angels are envious and "neither the angels in heaven above, nor the demons down under the sea, can ever dis**sever** my soul from the soul of the beautiful Annabel Lee".

See #169(1) USHER #317(1) STORY for #380(1)

#382 FLUFF
See #21(1) DEATH #369(2) BRINK

#384 VOICE
See #253 CHANT for #384(2)

#385 STEAD
See #398 TRYST

#386 BERTH
See #355 GIRTH

#387 MADAM

*Limerick 387(1) is not original. It is one of my absolute favorites so I've included it.

See #251(1) VIVID #298(2) for #387(1)

#390 LIVER

See # 247(1) OTHER #307 PLANT #359(1+2) DONOR

394 FLOCK

*"Schlock" is Yiddish, meaning of low quality or value, trash.

See #166(1) CHEAT for #394(2)

#395 ANGRY

*_Look Back in Anger_ is a realist play written by English playwright John Osborne (1929-1994). It focuses on the life and marital struggles of an intelligent and educated but disaffected young man of working class origin, Jimmy Porter, and his equally competent yet impassive upper-middle-class wife, Alison. It was first performed in 1956. It was made into a film starring Richard Burton and Claire Bloom in 1959.

#397 APHID

See #399 MIDGE

#398 TRYST

*_Tristan and Isolde_ (or Iseult) is a medieval chivalric romance that has been retold in numerous variations since the 12th century. Based on a Celtic legend, the tale is a tragedy about an illicit love affair between the Cornish knight Tristan and the Irish princess Isolde. Their love is instigated by the ingestion of a love potion.

See #385 STEAD

#399 MIDGE

Aphid midges are tiny flies with long, slender legs. There are 60 different species of aphids that attack vegetable crops, ornamentals and fruit trees. Midges are very effective in managing aphid infestation.

See #279(2) DEPOT #397 APHID

WORDLE LIMERICKS – INDEX

NUMBER	WORDLE	CATEGORY NO.	NO. OF LIMERICKS	CROSS REFERENCE
0	CIGAR	26	1	290
1	REBUT	2,12	1	35(2)
2	SISSY	24	1	
3	HUMPH	7	1	87
4	AWAKE	18	1	
5	BLUSH	24	2	
6	FOCAL	4,16	1	
7	EVADE	13	1	169(1)
8	NAVAL	21,26	1	
9	SERVE	21,24	2	
10	HEATH	6	1	
11	DWARF	8,20	1	101
12	MODEL	16,32	1	
13	KARMA	8,13,18	3	
14	STINK	32	1	
15	GRADE	33	1	
16	QUIET	8,17,21	2	
17	BENCH	32	1	
18	ABATE	8,20	2	45,110
19	FEIGN	24	1	
20	MAJOR	18,21,22,23	3	59(2)
21	DEATH	7,11,14,17	2	369(2),382
22	FRESH	8,18	1	
23	CRUST	20	1	
24	STOOL	2,30	1	
25	COLON	8,10,20	1	
26	ABASE	6	1	
27	MARRY	18	1	

NUMBER	WORDLE	CATEGORY NO.	NO. OF LIMERICKS	CROSS REFERENCE
28	REACT	24,31	2	
29	BATTY	27	1	
30	PRIDE	6,17	2	159(2)
31	FLOSS	20,24	1	
32	HELIX	20,30	1	
33	CROAK	6	1	
34	STAFF	1	1	
35	PAPER	2,4,12	2	1
36	UNFED	24	1	
37	WHELP	1	1	90
38	TRAWL	18,30	1	
39	OUTDO	6,18	1	57
40	ADOBE	9,33	1	
41	CRAZY	11,22,30	2	
42	SOWER	17	1	
43	REPAY	6,24	1	
44	DIGIT	30	1	
45	CRATE	33	1	18,110
46	CLUCK	24	1	
47	SPIKE	11,18,26	2	
48	MIMIC	20	1	
49	POUND	8,13	2	
50	MAXIM	10	1	
51	LINEN	11,16	1	216
52	UNMET	18,20	1	
53	FLESH	8,20	1	
54	BOOBY	18,21	2	271(1)
55	FORTH	9	1	
56	FIRST	11,22	1	
57	STAND	11,21	1	39(2)
58	BELLY	8,20	1	103
59	IVORY	1,4,8,16	2	20(3)
60	SEEDY	24	1	
61	PRINT	3,4	2	

NUMBER	WORDLE	CATEGORY NO.	NO. OF LIMERICKS	CROSS REFERENCE
62	YEARN	18,32	2	
63	DRAIN	9,20,23,30	2	
64	BRIBE	24	1	
65	STOUT	8,20	2	
66	PANEL	4	1	201
67	CRASS	24	1	
68	FLUME	9,11	1	
69	OFFAL	8	1	
70	AGREE	18,29	1	
71	ERROR	6	1	
72	SWIRL	8,20	1	
73	ARGUE	4,18	1	
74	BLEED	13	1	
75	DELTA	19,33	2	
76	FLICK	4,22,32	2	
77	TOTEM	1,7,20,21	2	
78	WOOER	27	1	
79	FRONT	4,26	2	
80	SHRUB	1	1	
81	PARRY	18,31	1	
82	BIOME	15,20	1	
83	LAPEL	16,24	1	257(2)
84	START	18	2	158
85	GREET	18,27,29	2	
86	GONER	14	1	
87	GOLEM	7,31	1	3
88	LUSTY	18,32	2	
89	LOOPY	22,27,32	2	
90	ROUND	1,17	1	37
91	AUDIT	26	1	
92	LYING	18	1	
93	GAMMA	1,8,9,10,30	2	160(1),179(1),277(1)
94	LABOR	4,20	2	
95	ISLET	8,20	1	

NUMBER	WORDLE	CATEGORY NO.	NO. OF LIMERICKS	CROSS REFERENCE
96	CIVIC	4,11,26	1	
97	FORGE	4,11,18	2	
98	CORNY	10,18	2	
99	MOULT	1,20	2	315
100	BASIC	8,21,25,28,30	2	
101	SALAD	1,8	1	11
102	AGATE	4,16	1	
103	SPICY	8,32	2	58
104	SPRAY	20	1	
105	ESSAY	5	1	
106	FJORD	9	1	
107	SPEND	17,18,24	2	202(2)
108	KEBAB	8	1	
109	GUILD	13,22	2	
110	ABACK	11,21	1	18,45
111	MOTOR	20,23,27	2	
112	ALONE	23,24	2	
113	HATCH	18	1	
114	HYPER	7	1	
115	THUMB	7,9,24	3	
116	DOWRY	18	1	
117	OUGHT	29	1	
118	BELCH	20	1	
119	DUTCH	9,18	2	
120	PILOT	33	1	
121	TWEED	4,8,11,24,27	2	
122	COMET	17,30	1	290
123	JAUNT	9,18	1	
124	ENEMA	20,32	1	
125	STEED	1,7	1	
126	ABYSS	20,27	1	
127	GROWL	1,20	1	
128	FLING	16,18	1	164(2),285
129	DOZEN	4,13,19,21,22	2	

NUMBER	WORDLE	CATEGORY NO.	NO. OF LIMERICKS	CROSS REFERENCE
130	BOOZY	8,24	2	
131	ERODE	30	1	
132	WORLD	28,30	2	
133	GOUGE	7,17	1	
134	CLICK	13,18,21,32	2	
135	BRIAR	1,17	1	
136	GREAT	13,18,27	2	163,187(2)
137	ALTAR	18	1	
138	PULPY	8,18,20	2	
139	BLURT	20,28	1	
140	COAST	8,27	1	
141	DUCHY	29	2	289
142	GROIN	20,27	1	
143	FIXER	18	1	
144	GROUP	18,23,32	2	339
145	ROGUE	1,11,22	1	
146	BADLY	18	1	
147	SMART	20,24,25	2	
148	PITHY	1,22	1	
149	GAUDY	6,16,24	1	
150	CHILL	23,27	2	
151	HERON	1,8	2	378
152	VODKA	24,27,31	1	
153	FINER	18,32	1	
154	SURER	18,31	1	
155	RADIO	23,30	2	
156	ROUGE	16,22,30	1	
157	PERCH	1,8,28	2	
158	RETCH	20,30,32	1	
159	WROTE	17	2	30(2)
160	CLOCK	1,7,30	2	93(2),179(1)
161	TILDE	10,19	2	
162	STORE	7,21	2	
163	PROVE	30	1	136(2)

NUMBER	WORDLE	CATEGORY NO.	NO. OF LIMERICKS	CROSS REFERENCE
164	BRING	7,32	2	128,236,285
165	SOLVE	4,17	2	
166	CHEAT	17,22,23,28	2	
167	GRIME	9,10,23	1	168,394(2)
168	EXULT	14,27	1	
169	USHER	9,14,17,23	3	166(1),394(2)
170	EPOCH	11,30	2	
171	TRIAD	23,28	2	
172	BREAK	20,21,30	2	
173	RHINO	1,26	2	
174	VIRAL	1,15,20,26	2	
175	CONIC	19	1	
176	MASSE	22,31	1	
177	SONIC	20,23,30	2	
178	VITAL	7,21,30	2	
179	TRACE	1,20,30	2	93(2),160(1),
180	USING	18,20	1	
181	PEACH	3,8	1	74
182	CHAMP	22,26.31	2	
183	BATON	8,31	2	
184	BRAKE	1,27,30	2	
185	PLUCK	1,8,33	2	
186	CRAZE	5	1	
187	GRIPE	22,24,26,31	2	136(2)
188	WEARY	8,18	2	
189	PICKY	18,27,32	2	
190	ACUTE	6,19,27	2	
191	FERRY	7,14	1	
192	ASIDE	4,14,17,18,	2	
193	TAPIR	1,	2	
194	TROLL	7,27,30	2	219(1)
195	UNIFY	11,30	1	
196	REBUS	10,19	1	
197	BOOST	18	1	

NUMBER	WORDLE	CATEGORY NO.	NO. OF LIMERICKS	CROSS REFERENCE
198	TRUSS	6,8,20	2	259(1)
199	SIEGE	8,13	1	
200	TIGER	1,7,10,17	2	
201	BANAL	7,12,30	1	66
202	SLUMP	17,24,31	2	
203	CRANK	30	1	
204	GORGE	8,20,28	1	
205	QUERY	28,30	1	
206	DRINK	4,8,15,16,18,20	3	
207	FAVOR	4,18,31	2	
208	ABBEY	27,28	1	
209	TANGY	8	1	
210	PANIC	7,13,22,27	2	
211	SOLAR	9,18,22,30	2	
212	SHIRE	7,22	1	
213	PROXY	33	1	
214	POINT	19,27,33	2	
215	ROBOT	17,22,30	2	
216	PRICK	7,32	2	51
217	WINCE	7,8,28	2	
218	CRIMP	1,16,18	2	
219	KNOLL	4,11,18,26	2	194(1)
220	SUGAR	8,20	1	
221	WHACK	19,33	2	
222	MOUNT	9,12,32	3	
223	PERKY	20,27	1	
224	COULD	10,27	2	
225	WRUNG	18,27	1	
226	LIGHT	8,30	2	
227	THOSE	10	1	
228	MOIST	6	1	
229	SHARD	22	1	
230	PLEAT	16,24	1	
231	ALOFT	6,20	1	

NUMBER	WORDLE	CATEGORY NO.	NO. OF LIMERICKS	CROSS REFERENCE
232	SKILL	1,8	1	
233	ELDER	28	1	
234	FRAME	4,30	2	
235	HUMOR	8,20,27	2	
236	PAUSE	7	1	164
237	ULCER	15,20	2	
238	ULTRA	13,26	1	
239	ROBIN	1,28	1	248(1),260
240	CYNIC	12,25	1	
241	AROMA	1,8	2	
242	CAULK	9	1	
243	SHAKE	8,20,23	2	
244	DODGE	13,17,22	2	
245	SWILL	8	2	
246	TACIT	18	1	
247	OTHER	6,20,30	2	307,359(1+2),390(1)
248	THORN	1,28	2	239(1),260
249	TROVE	4	1	
250	BLOKE	20,27	1	
251	VIVID	27,28	2	298(2),387(1)
252	SPILL	1,13,26	2	
253	CHANT	23,28	1	384(2)
254	CHOKE	18,22,32	2	
255	RUPEE	19,26	1	
256	NASTY	13,20,23	2	
257	MOURN	23,28	2	83
258	AHEAD	10,27	2	
259	BRINE	8,12	2	198(2)
260	CLOTH	28,30	1	
261	HOARD	1,27,28	1	
262	SWEET	8,20,23,31	2	
263	MONTH	10,19,27,30,33	3	
264	LAPSE	8,18,27,29	2	
265	WATCH	11,21,24	2	

NUMBER	WORDLE	CATEGORY NO.	NO. OF LIMERICKS	CROSS REFERENCE
266	TODAY	6,27	2	
267	FOCUS	20,30	2	
268	SMELT	1,7,30	2	
269	TEASE	7,22,32	2	
270	CATER	1,8	1	
271	MOVIE	18,22,30	2	54(2)
272	SAUTE	8	1	284
273	ALLOW	7,20,27	2	
274	RENEW	20,30	1	
275	THEIR	3,10	1	
276	SLOSH	9	1	
277	PURGE	1,8,20,27,28	2	93(1)
278	CHEST	16,20,27	2	
279	DEPOT	15,20,21	2	
280	EPOXY	30	1	399
281	NYMPH	1,7,15	2	210(2)
282	FOUND	1,8,16,18	2	
283	SHALL	10,28	1	
284	STOVE	8	1	272
285	LOWLY	7,18,29	1	128,164(2)
286	SNOUT	7,17,22	3	
287	TROPE	10	1	
288	FEWER	10,19	1	
289	SHAWL	6,16,18,32	1	141(2),169(2)
290	NATAL	17,30	1	0,122
291	COMMA	6,10,20	1	
292	FORAY	10,13,21	1	
293	SCARE	14,18,22	2	
294	STAIR	6,24,32	2	
295	BLACK	1,4,6,11,22,26	4	
296	SQUAD	21,26	2	
297	ROYAL	29	1	
298	CHUNK	9,18,28,30	2	251(1),387(1)
299	MINCE	8,29,33	2	

NUMBER	WORDLE	CATEGORY NO.	NO. OF LIMERICKS	CROSS REFERENCE
300	SHAME	23,27	2	
301	CHEEK	5,20,33	2	
302	AMPLE	18,20,31	2	
303	FLAIR	8,20	1	
304	FOYER	18	1	
305	CARGO	21,26	1	
306	OXIDE	30	1	
307	PLANT	20	1	247(1),359(1+2),390(1)
308	OLIVE	8,22,23	3	
309	INERT	1,20,30	3	
310	ASKEW	3	1	
311	HEIST	4	1	
312	SHOWN	32	1	
313	ZESTY	8	1	
314	TRASH	6,18	2	
315	LARVA	15	1	99
316	FORGO	28,31	2	
317	STORY	6,7,14,17	2	169(1),380(1)
318	HAIRY	7,14,15,20	2	
319	TRAIN	1,6,27	2	
320	HOMER	17,31	1	359(2)
321	BADGE	16,17,21,24,28	2	
322	MIDST	21,26	1	
323	CANNY	3,4	1	
324	SHINE	18,30	2	
325	GECKO	1,3,7	2	
326	FARCE	17	1	
327	SLUNG	10,28	1	
328	TIPSY	18,27	2	
329	METAL	7,14,16,30	2	
330	YIELD	4	1	
331	DELVE	18,23,27	2	
332	BEING	10,17,27,28,31	2	
333	SCOUR	7,17	1	

NUMBER	WORDLE	CATEGORY NO.	NO. OF LIMERICKS	CROSS REFERENCE
334	GLASS	23,30	2	
335	GAMER	20,27	1	
336	SCRAP	1	1	
337	MONEY	12,26	2	
338	HINGE	20,31	1	
339	ALBUM	8,23	1	144(1)
340	VOUCH	24,27	1	
341	ASSET	18	1	
342	TIARA	1,15,16,33	2	
343	CREPT	1,17,32	2	
344	BAYOU	1,10,11	3	
345	ATOLL	9,17	2	
346	MANOR	1,8,17,18	4	
347	CREAK	20,33	2	
348	SHOWY	16,27,31	2	
349	PHASE	6,30	2	
350	FROTH	8,12,20	2	
351	DEPTH	9	1	
352	GLOOM	13,14	2	
353	FLOOD	11,28	2	
354	TRAIT	10.24	2	
355	GIRTH	9,19	1	55,386
356	PIETY	8,28	1	
357	GOOSE	1,24,30	2	358(1)
358	FLOAT	12,18,30	2	357(1)
359	DONOR	12,17,20,27	2	247(1),307,390(1)
360	ATONE	4,20	2	
361	PRIMO	6	1	
362	APRON	8,32	2	
363	BLOWN	3,9	2	
364	CACAO	8,20,30	2	
365	LOSER	18	1	
366	INPUT	20,30	1	
367	GLOAT	27	1	

NUMBER	WORDLE	CATEGORY NO.	NO. OF LIMERICKS	CROSS REFERENCE
368	AWFUL	1,15,27	2	
369	BRINK	11,13,17	2	21(1),382
370	SMITE	28	2	
371	BEADY	4,27	1	
372	RUSTY	18,20	2	
373	RETRO	6,16	1	
374	DROLL	24	1	
375	GAWKY	24	1	
376	HUTCH	6,13	1	
377	PINTO	1,8	1	
378	EGRET	1,10,30	1	151(2)
379	LILAC	30	2	
380	SEVER	17,18,20	2	169(1),317(1)
381	FIELD	1,26	2	
382	FLUFF	4,17	1	21(1),369(2)
383	AGAPE	1,27,32	2	
384	VOICE	18,23	2	253
385	STEAD	32	1	398
386	BERTH	20,30	1	355
387	MADAM	20,28,32	2	251(1),298(2)
388	NIGHT	1,20,27,30	2	
389	BLAND	8,18	2	
390	LIVER	2,20	2	247(1),307,359(1+2)
391	WEDGE	27,33	2	
392	ROOMY	32	1	
393	WACKY	27	1	
394	FLOCK	1,7,10,28	2	
395	ANGRY	18,22,26,27	2	
396	TRITE	27,30	1	
397	APHID	15	1	399
398	TRYST	7,17,18	1	385
399	MIDGE	15,20	1	397
400	POWER	19,26	2	

WORDLE LIMERICKS – ALPHABETICAL ORDER

WORDLE	NUMBER
ABACK	110
ABASE	26
ABATE	18
ABBEY	208
ABYSS	126
ACUTE	190
ADOBE	40
AGAPE	383
AGATE	102
AGREE	70
AHEAD	258
ALBUM	339
ALLOW	273
ALOFT	231
ALONE	112
ALTAR	137
AMPLE	302
ANGRY	395
APHID	397
APRON	362
ARGUE	73
AROMA	241
ASIDE	192
ASKEW	310
ASSET	341
ATOLL	345
ATONE	360
AUDIT	91
AWAKE	4

WORDLE	NUMBER
AWFUL	368
BADGE	321
BADLY	146
BANAL	201
BASIC	100
BATON	183
BATTY	29
BAYOU	344
BEADY	371
BEING	332
BELCH	118
BELLY	58
BENCH	17
BERTH	386
BIOME	82
BLACK	295
BLAND	389
BLEED	74
BLOKE	250
BLOWN	363
BLURT	139
BLUSH	5
BOOBY	54
BOOST	197
BOOZY	130
BRAKE	184
BREAK	172
BRIAR	135
BRIBE	64

WORDLE	NUMBER	WORDLE	NUMBER
BRINE	259	CREPT	343
BRING	164	CRIMP	218
BRINK	369	CROAK	33
CACAO	364	CRUST	23
CANNY	323	CYNIC	240
CARGO	305	DEATH	21
CATER	270	DELTA	75
CAULK	242	DELVE	331
CHAMP	182	DEPOT	279
CHANT	253	DEPTH	351
CHEAT	166	DIGIT	44
CHEEK	301	DODGE	244
CHEST	278	DONOR	359
CHILL	150	DOWRY	116
CHOKE	254	DOZEN	129
CHUNK	298	DRAIN	63
CIGAR	0	DRINK	206
CIVIC	96	DROLL	374
CLICK	134	DUCHY	141
CLOCK	160	DUTCH	119
CLOTH	260	DWARF	11
CLUCK	46	EGRET	378
COAST	140	ELDER	233
COLON	25	ENEMA	124
COMET	122	EPOCH	170
COMMA	291	EPOXY	280
CONIC	175	ERODE	131
CORNY	98	ERROR	71
COULD	224	ESSAY	105
CRANK	203	EVADE	7
CRASS	67	EXULT	168
CRATE	45	FARCE	326
CRAZE	186	FAVOR	207
CRAZY	41	FEIGN	19
CREAK	347	FERRY	191

WORDLE	NUMBER	WORDLE	NUMBER
FEWER	288	GLOAT	367
FIELD	381	GLOOM	352
FINER	153	GOLEM	3
FIRST	56	GOLEM	87
FIXER	143	GONER	86
FJORD	106	GOOSE	357
FLAIR	303	GORGE	204
FLESH	53	GOUGE	133
FLICK	76	GRADE	15
FLING	128	GREAT	136
FLOAT	358	GREET	85
FLOCK	394	GRIME	167
FLOOD	353	GRIPE	187
FLOSS	31	GROIN	142
FLUFF	382	GROUP	144
FLUME	68	GROWL	127
FOCAL	6	GUILD	109
FOCUS	267	HAIRY	318
FORAY	292	HATCH	113
FORGE	97	HEATH	10
FORGO	316	HEIST	311
FORTH	55	HELIX	32
FOUND	282	HERON	151
FOYER	304	HINGE	338
FRAME	234	HOARD	261
FRESH	22	HOMER	320
FRONT	79	HUMOR	235
FROTH	350	HUMPH	3
GAMER	335	HUTCH	376
GAMMA	93	HYPER	114
GAUDY	149	INERT	309
GAWKY	375	INPUT	366
GECKO	325	ISLET	95
GIRTH	355	IVORY	59
GLASS	334	JAUNT	123

WORDLE	NUMBER	WORDLE	NUMBER
KARMA	13	MOVIE	271
KEBAB	108	NASTY	256
KNOLL	219	NATAL	290
LABOR	94	NAVAL	8
LAPEL	83	NIGHT	388
LAPSE	264	NYMPH	281
LARVA	315	OFFAL	69
LIGHT	226	OLIVE	308
LILAC	379	OTHER	247
LINEN	51	OUGHT	117
LIVER	390	OUTDO	39
LOOPY	89	OXIDE	306
LOSER	365	PANEL	66
LOWLY	285	PANIC	210
LUSTY	88	PAPER	35
LYING	92	PARRY	81
MADAM	387	PAUSE	236
MAJOR	20	PEACH	181
MANOR	346	PERCH	157
MARRY	27	PERKY	223
MASSE	176	PHASE	349
MAXIM	50	PICKY	189
METAL	329	PIETY	356
MIDGE	399	PILOT	120
MIDST	322	PINTO	377
MIMIC	48	PITHY	148
MINCE	299	PLANT	307
MODEL	12	PLEAT	230
MOIST	228	PLUCK	185
MONEY	337	POINT	214
MONTH	263	POUND	49
MOTOR	111	POWER	400
MOULT	99	PRICK	216
MOUNT	222	PRIDE	30
MOURN	257	PRIMO	361

WORDLE	NUMBER
PRINT	61
PROVE	163
PROXY	213
PULPY	138
PURGE	277
QUERY	205
QUIET	16
RADIO	155
REACT	28
REBUS	196
REBUT	1
RENEW	274
REPAY	43
RETCH	158
RETRO	373
RHINO	173
ROBIN	239
ROBOT	215
ROGUE	145
ROOMY	392
ROUGE	156
ROUND	90
ROYAL	297
RUPEE	255
RUSTY	372
SALAD	101
SAUTE	272
SCARE	293
SCOUR	333
SCRAP	336
SEEDY	60
SERVE	9
SEVER	380
SHAKE	243
SHALL	283

WORDLE	NUMBER
SHAME	300
SHARD	229
SHAWL	289
SHINE	324
SHIRE	212
SHOWN	312
SHOWY	348
SHRUB	80
SIEGE	199
SISSY	2
SKILL	232
SLOSH	276
SLUMP	202
SLUNG	327
SMART	147
SMELT	268
SMITE	370
SNOUT	286
SOLAR	211
SOLVE	165
SONIC	177
SOWER	42
SPEND	107
SPICY	103
SPIKE	47
SPILL	252
SPRAY	104
SQUAD	296
STAFF	34
STAIR	294
STAND	57
START	84
STEAD	385
STEED	125
STINK	14

WORDLE	NUMBER	WORDLE	NUMBER
STOOL	24	TRYST	398
STORE	162	TWEED	121
STORY	317	ULCER	237
STOUT	65	ULTRA	238
STOVE	284	UNFED	36
SUGAR	220	UNIFY	195
SURER	154	UNMET	52
SWEET	262	USHER	169
SWILL	245	USING	180
SWIRL	72	VIRAL	174
TACIT	246	VITAL	178
TANGY	209	VIVID	251
TAPIR	193	VODKA	152
TEASE	269	VOICE	384
THEIR	275	VOUCH	340
THORN	248	WACKY	393
THOSE	227	WATCH	265
THUMB	115	WEARY	188
TIARA	342	WEDGE	391
TIGER	200	WHACK	221
TILDE	161	WHELP	37
TIPSY	328	WINCE	217
TODAY	266	WOOER	78
TOTEM	77	WORLD	132
TRACE	179	WROTE	159
TRAIN	319	WRUNG	225
TRAIT	354	YEARN	62
TRASH	314	YIELD	330
TRAWL	38	ZESTY	313
TRIAD	171		
TRITE	396		
TROLL	194		
TROPE	287		
TROVE	249		
TRUSS	198		

ACKNOWLEDGEMENTS

The Wordle Limerick book evolved with the help of many friends and family members:

My stepdaughter, Carolina Simunovic, introduced me and nurtured my addiction to the game of Wordle, which clearly was the first step involved in the creation of this book. My wonderful wife, Ximena Navarrete Flam, frequently provided helpful feedback and tolerated my readings of the daily limericks. She was also the person who suggested I publish the limericks.

My small group of fans with whom I shared my daily limericks were an inspiration providing appreciative feedback which greatly encouraged my efforts. This group included: my beautiful granddaughter Ralph (Holly) Black who was incredibly helpful in editing. Her input into this reedited version of Volume 1 resulted in a significant improvement in the quality of the limericks and added many additional 6th lines. Additionally, the president of my fan club, Dina Kassel, the vice president of my fan club Stacy Batrich Smith, my daughter Danielle Flam, my sister Andrea Moskowitz, my grandson Cameron Black, and my friend Lynn Crandall.

There were many individuals whom I forced myself upon to read my limericks to. Some were welcoming, others tolerant, while others were marginally receptive to non-receptive. Many thanks to all but the last group. While there are too many of these tolerant individuals to mention, my special thanks go to my daughters Gabrielle Cummins, Carley Decker, Shari Flam, and Arielle Mitton. Others whom I pushed beyond their tolerance to be receptive include Omar Sanchez, Isa Simunovic-Munoz, Andrew Mitton, Alfie Cummins, Terry Smith, Giuliano Morse, Tony Chacon, Larry Gittens, Mary Therese Kerrigan, Maria Marzullo, David Gardner and Paul Cummins.

www.ingramcontent.com/pod-product-compliance
Lightning Source LLC
LaVergne TN
LVHW061933070526
838199LV00060B/3833